Taboo, Magic, Spirits

Taboo, Magic, Spirits
A study of primitive elements in Roman religion
Author: Eli Edward Burriss

Original publication: 1931
Cover image: *Circe Offering the Cup to Ulysses* (1891) by John William Waterhouse (1849-1917)
Lay-out: www.burokd.nl

ISBN 978-94-92355-03-4

© 2015 Revised publication by:

VAMzzz Publishing
P.O. Box 3340
1001 AC Amsterdam
The Netherlands
www.vamzzz.com
contactvamzzz@gmail.com

TABOO, MAGIC
SPIRITS
A Study of Primitive Elements in Roman Religion

Eli Edward Burriss

VAMzzz PUBLISHING

contents

PREFACE   9

CHAPTER I   Mana, Magic and Animism   13
  The Mind of Primitive Man—13   Positive and Negative Mana—18
  Magic—22   Animism—23

CHAPTER II   Positive and Negative Mana (Taboo)   29
  Blood—31   Women—40   Children—43
  Death and Corpses—60   Leather—64   Days—65

CHAPTER III   Miscellaneous Taboos   69
  Sex—69   Men—75   Strangers —77
  Slaves—80   Linen and Wool—81   Knots—85
  Iron and Bronze—88   Places—92

CHAPTER IV   Magic Acts: The General Principles   95
  Homoeopathic and Contagious Magic—95

CHAPTER V   Removing Evils by Magic Acts   109
  Removing the Evil Effects of Dangerous Contact by Washing and
  Burning—113
  Removing Evils by Sweeping and Striking—117
  Keeping Away Evils by Drawing a Magic Circle—123
  Removing Evils by Dancing: The Scapegoat—127

CHAPTER VI Incantation and Prayer   *133*

Prayer a Command—*136*   Prayers Chanted—*137*

Prayers Uttered in an Undervoice—*138*

Prayers Repeated—*139*

Exactness in Naming the God and in the Wording of the Prayer—*140*

Prayers for Ill—*141*

No God Involved—*143*

CHAPTER VII Naturalism and Animism   *147*

The Worship of Stones—*148*   Trees and Groves—*151*

Water—*158*   Fire—*167*

VAMzzz Publishing - More Occult and Esoteric Books

PREFACE

ROMAN RELIGION, as we meet it in historical times, is a congeries of many elements. One of the problems of the modern scholar is to separate and interpret these various elements—primitive, Latin, Etruscan, Greek, Oriental. Even the casual student of comparative religion, who is also familiar with Latin literature, cannot fail to recognize, running through the enormous mass of facts and ideas about religion and superstition, elements which are common to all religions, past and present, whether among savages or civilized men. Such elements, when discovered in a developed religion, may fairly be called primitive. In the study of the religion of any people, the starting point should be with these common elements.

However, it has usually been the habit of scholars to trace the development of gods and goddesses, rites and priesthoods, to their historical sources, and to describe and interpret the Roman calendar with its many festivals; and if primitive elements have been treated at all, they have formed part of a larger work, or have been rather cursorily dismissed to clear the way for a study of the religion of the organized Roman State. Thus W. Warde Fowler, in *The Roman Festivals of the Period of the Republic,* and Georg Wissowa, in his *Religion und Kultus der Romer,* were concerned primarily with the facts of historical Roman religion. Fowler, to be sure, devoted two chapters in *The Religious Experience of the Roman People* to a study of primitive elements, but he was clearly anxious to hurry on to his main theme. H. J. Rose, in his *Primitive Culture in Italy,* has discussed briefly, but with sound scholarship, primitive elements in Roman religion as part of the general subject of primitive culture in Italy; and Jesse Benedict Carter, following afar his master Wissowa, seems to have had slender knowledge of comparative religion. To Sir J. G. Frazer scholars owe much for his valuable collection of rites and ideas parallel to those of the Romans. *The Golden Bough* is a veritable mine of such information; and the author's more recent work, his edition of the *Fasti of Ovid,* is indispensable to the student of the subject. The latter reached my hands after I had completed the first draft of my manuscript for publication. Because of the pertinence of his notes on the passages from Ovid's Fasti which I have used in this work, I have included in the footnotes references to Frazer's work wherever possible.

No one has as yet, so far as I know, made an attempt to gather from the ancient sources those elements in the Roman State religion and in the popular religious life of the Roman people which are commonly termed primitive. Eugene Tavenner, in his *Studies in Magic from Latin Literature,* has given us a valuable body of facts about magic, but has made little effort to interpret the material.

It is obviously difficult, and in many cases impossible, to determine what elements are truly primitive and what are not. There are certain traces which are unmistakably primitive. These I have treated at length: positive and negative mana, the principles of sympathetic magic, naturalism, and animism. I shall discuss more fully certain subjects which have grown out of my study of the primitive elements, and of which a knowledge is necessary for the understanding of these elements.

Most of the excerpts in this work have been obtained from a first-hand reading, over a period of five years, of the original sources. Some of this material was published, perhaps prematurely, in various periodicals, *Classical Philology, The Classical Journal, The Classical Weekly, The Biblical Review, Art and Archaeology.* It was only after I had gathered and classified and interpreted as best I could alone that I turned to the secondary sources. My debt both to these and to the original is indicated in the footnotes.

The translations are, except in one case, my own. I have adopted Frazer's practice of translating into English the names of festivals wherever these names could not be readily understood by the reader who was not classically trained.

It remains to thank my associates, Professor Casper J. Kraemer Jr., and Miss Catherine Ruth Smith, for many helpful suggestions in preparing the manuscript.

Eli Edward Burriss, New York
April, 1931

CHAPTER I

Mana, Magic and Animism

The Mind of Primitive Man

EARLY MAN, in common with present-day savages, was unable to form correct inferences concerning the world about him. The reason for this seems to lie in the ignorance and in the intensely powerful imagination of the savage, which make him unable to distinguish truth from error. This characteristic, in turn, may be due to the fact that the brain of the savage is not developed enough physiologically to enable him to form correct associations and to draw correct inferences. Furthermore, the imaginings of the savage are heightened by his precarious life and by the intensity of the dangers which beset him in his struggle to survive. This inability to think correctly led, for instance, to the feeling that blood possessed peculiar and dangerous properties—a feeling extremely common among savages, and, for that matter, even among civilized persons.

So in the old Roman days Titus Manlius, having killed a gigantic Gaul in a hand-to-hand conflict, cut off the Gaul's head, "wrenched off his necklace and placed it, reeking with blood, on his own neck." From that time on he and his descendants bore the surname Torquatus (torques—a chain or necklace). [1] The family of Torquatus had the necklace as a device down to the time of the Emperor Caligula, who forbade its use. [2] Again, in a much later time, during one of the pagan persecutions, a Christian, Saturus, was thrown to the leopards. A single gnash of the wild beast bathed him in blood. Turning to a soldier who was also, but in secret, a Christian, he asked for the ring which he was wearing; and when the soldier gave it to him, he smeared it with his own lifeblood and handed it back. [3]

These are not merely the actions of a bloodthirsty soldier, crazed with victory, and of a religious fanatic. It was the inability to think correctly that caused Torquatus to place the gory necklace of his slain opponent about his own neck, and that impelled Saturus to smear the ring of his fellow Christian with his own blood and hand it back to him.

The curious twist in thinking which produced these actions has been considered a characteristic of the so-called age of magic; but it is by no means limited to that theoretical period, nor, indeed, to the savage, for it may be found to-day among children and even among adults. Thus a four-year-old child came running to her kindergarten teacher in a fright, sobbing out, "The sky barked at me!" [4] The child had observed the barking of a dog; the sky made a noise which seemed to her exactly like it. Hence she felt that the sky was like a dog, if not actually a dog.

In his capacity as a minister my father frequently had occasion to christen children, sprinkling them with water. One of his parishioners, on returning from a visit to Palestine, brought back a gallon of water from the Jordan. The members of the parish, learning of this, made frequent requests that this water be used to sprinkle their children at christening ceremonies. Had anyone asked them why they wanted their children christened with Jordan water, they would probably have been quite at a loss, or else have suggested some sentimental reason or other. But their actions, if analyzed, might have yielded the following process of reasoning: Christ was baptized in the Jordan two thousand years ago; the Jordan is, therefore, a holy river. Water from the Jordan, having been in contact with Christ, is equal to Christ, so far, at least, as its sanctifying effects are concerned. Therefore children who are sprinkled with water from the Jordan come in contact with Christ.

No one would assert that the child, before crying out that the sky barked at her, went through any conscious process of thinking. No more did Torquatus reason when he smeared the necklace with the blood of his Gallic foe. But their actions can only be analyzed by tracing the faulty and unconscious line of reasoning upon which they were based. Folk stories abound in similar actions, capable of analysis on the basis of the modes of thinking of an educated man.

This primitive type of reasoning leads a person to believe, for instance, that a thing which has been in contact with another thing is still in contact with it, however far removed it may be in reality. This may be referred to as the principle of contact.

In the Attic Nights of Gellius [5] we read that, if a dispute involving land was to be settled, the disputants, together with the judge, were compelled to go to the land involved and "lay hands" on the property. With the growth of Italy, however, the judges found it inconvenient to leave Rome to "lay hands" on the actual property; so the disputants would visit the land, returning with a clod of earth taken from it, and perform at Rome the necessary "laying on" of hands, just as if present on the land itself.

Apuleius preserves for us [6] the story of Thelyphron, who lost his nose and ears in a most remarkable manner. On his arrival at Larissa on the way to the Olympian Games, he rambled about the streets, seeking some means of bettering his fortunes. Presently he heard an old man in the market place crying out at the top of his voice: "If anyone is willing to keep watch over a corpse, he shall receive a reward." Thelyphron inquired the reason for this strange request. "In Thessaly," the old man said, "witches bite off pieces here and there from the faces of the dead, and with these they reinforce their magic arts." He further revealed how witches would often change themselves into birds, or dogs, or mice, or even flies, and thereby accomplish their nefarious ends. He then added these significant words: "If anyone shall fail to restore the corpse untouched in the morning, whatever has been snatched from it shall be snatched from his own face to patch up the face of the corpse." Thelyphron agreed, even in the teeth of this knowledge, to watch over the dead man, for he was sorely in need of money. He fell asleep at his task: a witch, in the guise of a weasel, entered, tore off the nose and ears of the dead man and replaced them with wax. Next morning the widow, ignorant of the witch's trick, rewarded Thelyphron according to the agreement. But by a strange accident his fault was revealed. As the funeral cortege passed along the street, it was interrupted by an old man proclaiming that the deceased had been poisoned by his wife. In order to ascertain the truth concerning this murder, an Egyptian soothsayer was consulted. In bringing the dead man to life for a moment, he incidentally revealed the witch's stratagem. Thelyphron, realizing that, according to the superstition, he must lose his ears and nose, felt for these members, and they instantly fell off. According to the original rite, Thelyphron's nose and ears would have been cut off, presumably by a member of the dead man's family; but in Apuleius' retelling, the parts which the corpse had lost the man lost by sheer sympathetic magic.

During the Middle Ages Rome suffered from a plague of flies. Vergil, who, as the people believed, often came back as a wonder-working wizard, was called upon to rid the city of the pests. As the story goes, he consulted Il Moscone, the king of the flies, and at his suggestion caused a great golden image of a fly to be set up, which miraculously drove the pests from the city. [7] This illustrates the axiom that "like cures like," a principle which magic and medicine have in common.

The Romans themselves had some inkling of the principles involved in such stories as these. Cicero, for example, writes: [8] "For, since bodies fell to earth, and these were covered with earth... men would think that the rest of the life of the dead was passed under the earth." Lucretius, in describing the struggles of primitive man, says: [9] "But in those times mankind was much hardier in the fields, as was fitting, because the earth which had produced them was hard." According to Ovid, [10] the reason why the Romans gave gifts of dates, figs and honey on New Year's Day was "that the year might in sweetness go through the course which it had begun." Apuleius, in his defense against the charge of using a certain fish for magic purposes because of its indecent name and form, retorts: [11] "Tell me, is there anything more foolish than to infer from the similarity in the names of things that their force is identical?" And, finally, Servius writes: [12] "In sacrifices, likenesses are accepted for realities. Hence, when animals which are difficult to find must be sacrificed, they are made of bread or wax and are accepted as the real victims."

In all these instances there was some misconception, some inability to form inferences correctly; and in every case there has been an action performed in accordance with this misconception or incorrect inference. It did not, moreover, take modern anthropologists to discover this fact; the Romans themselves were conscious of it.

Positive and Negative Mana

Now religion seems to be the outgrowth of man's need to overcome the obstacles which nature places in his way in his struggle to survive. [13] Rain, drought, hail destroy his crops; lightning strikes his house; pestilence carries off his loved ones and his cattle. These evils, of whose origin he is ignorant, he must ward off, if he would survive; and he must, similarly, force the phenomena about him to do him good. In his effort to overcome these obstacles man reasons illogically much in the same way as the characters in our stories; or perhaps we should say, rather, that man's actions, from our viewpoint, suggest such illogical reasoning. For in most cases there has been no conscious process of thinking; or, if there has been any thinking, it is incomplete and hopelessly confused. Many of the superstitions, religious misconceptions and actions on the part of men grew out of this imperfect understanding of the facts of the universe, and out of man's inability to think correctly about these facts.

The ancients, as well as modern anthropologists, were aware

of the difficulties which primitive man had to encounter in his struggle to survive; and while the former were as yet unable to study these
problems scientifically, occasionally some of them like Lucretius
or Cicero would remark a principle, upon the discovery of which
modern anthropologists still plume themselves. Lucretius, the Roman
exponent of Epicureanism, anticipated many modern problems in
physical and social science. He has left us [14] a vividly imaginative
account of some of these early struggles of man:

"They neither knew how to treat things with fire nor how to
use the skins of wild animals to clothe their bodies; but they used
to live in groves and in the caves of mountains and in forests; and
they would hide their savage forms among the bushes, when driven
to avoid the lashing winds and rains... It caused them anxiety, poor
wretches, that wild creatures often made sleep fatal to them. Driven
out at the approach of the foaming wild boar and the powerful lion,
they would flee their rocky shelters; and in the depth of night, pan-
ic-stricken, they would often yield their leaf-strewn resting-places
to their wild guests. It was more likely then than now that mortal
men would leave the sweet light of ebbing life. For then each would
be seized and mangled by the teeth of wild beasts, furnishing them
with living food. All the while he would fill the groves, mountains, and
forests with his groans, beholding, as he did, his living vitals buried
in a living grave. But those whom flight had saved, although their
vitals were torn away, later, as they held their trembling hands over
their foul sores, would cry heartrendingly for death to take them; and
then their cruel gripings would separate them from life, helpless as
they were and ignorant of what was needed to heal their wounds...

In those days lack of food would bring death to their fainting limbs; in our times, on the contrary, it is overabundance which sinks them in ruin."

Cicero once wrote: [15] "Is it not as clear as day that the awe which early man felt because lightning and thunder had terrified him led him to believe that Jupiter, mighty in all things, caused these phenomena too?"

As soon as man becomes self-conscious, he feels that anything different from himself is potentially dangerous: it contains a mysterious power to do him harm and he must if possible compel it to do him good. If he finds by experience that it cannot do him good, but harm only, he must avoid it; and when this is impossible he must find some means to rid himself of the evil effects of contagion—usually by water or fire. Now he soon realizes that some things which are potentially dangerous—for example, rain, which brings floods and destruction in its wake—at times are beneficent; for rain may also cause his crops to grow and bring cooling showers after the heat of the day. However, other persons, things, or actions are found to be always harmful.

To this mysterious force, whether harmful or helpful, or potentially so, the name mana is given. [16] Mana which has been found to be always harmful is called taboo, and to this we choose to give the name negative mana. [17] Mana which has been found to be always good is usually called simply mana; but to this it seems better to give the name positive mana. Now there is no essential difference between a person, thing, or action possessing positive mana, which one compels by a magic act or a charm (or prayer) to do one's will, and the person, thing, or action which is as we say taboo, or which, to use our new term, possesses negative mana. In both cases there is, prior to experience with the person, action, or thing, potential danger or potential benefit inherent. In the case of negative mana the results of experience have shown that the danger is not only potential but actual; and in the case of positive mana experience has shown that potential good can be forced into actual good by a magic act. With negative mana or taboo the potential danger has been realized by experience to be actual, and so avoidance is necessary, or, if this is impossible, rites of purification must be performed to rid one's self of the evil of contagion.

A stranger possesses for the savage mind the peculiar property to which we have given the general name mana; he comes from the unexplored forest and may be harmful or helpful. When the stranger has attacked the savage, the latter realizes that the stranger possesses a power to harm (negative mana). When a second stranger comes from the woodland, the savage associates with him the harm done by the first stranger, and hence he has an uncanny feeling on seeing not only the stranger but anything which has been in contact with him, or, indeed, anything which has come from the same place as the stranger. If he cannot avoid the stranger and comes in contact with him or anything belonging to him, he must protect himself from the evil effects of contagion by a rite of purification. Hence, generals, soldiers, and their equipment must be purified before they enter the city on returning from a campaign, for they have been in unavoidable contact with their foes.

Magic

In the early stage of his development man has no conception of a superior being on whom he is dependent, whose will he must win; but he believes that by performing some mysterious action, usually imitating the action desired, and often assisted by an incantation or charm—whether it be an amulet for defense or a talisman for offense—he can force the desired result.

This mysterious action and incantation, passing under the name of magic, arises, as we have seen, from a curious twist in thinking which leads a person to believe that the effect is the same thing as the cause, that something like a person or thing is the person or thing itself, that similarity in thought is similarity in fact, and that something which has touched a person is still in contact with him.

When the individual imitates the action to be effected, anthropologists speak of homoeopathic magic; when he makes use of some object, such as clothes, hair, or nails, which has been a part of, or was in contact with, the individual, the name contagious magic is given. The general term sympathetic magic includes both types; for a mysterious sympathy is supposed to exist between the object to be influenced and the object which is like it or has been in contact with it. Often the same rite is both contagious and homoeopathic.

These definitions will become clearer in the following example, taken from a familiar rite of private magic.

The shepherdess in the song of Alphesiboeus, in Vergil's eighth Eclogue—which follows closely the second Idyll of Theocritus—essays to bring back her lover, Daphnis, by performing elaborate rites, accompanied by an incantation. In these magic rites, lustral water, sacred boughs, and frankincense are used. The homoeopathic element appears when the enchantress winds about the image of Daphnis three threads of different hues, in each of which is a knot; thus, as she binds the image of Daphnis, she hopes to bind Daphnis himself to his sweetheart, with the aid of an incantation, "Lead Daphnis home from the city, my charms, lead Daphnis home," repeated nine times during the rites. The enchantress employed two images of Daphnis, one of clay, representing him in his attitude toward other girls, toward whom he will harden as the clay hardens; the other, of wax, which melts and causes Daphnis to melt with love for his sweetheart. "As this clay hardens and this wax melts with one and the same fire," she sings, "so may Daphnis melt with my love." In these rites, some personal effects which Daphnis has left behind are hidden by the witch in the earth under the threshold. As she buries them, she addresses the earth: "These relics, O Earth, I entrust to thee. These pledges are bound to give me Daphnis." This element in the rites is "contagious," since the objects had once been in contact with Daphnis.

Animism

We now turn to another subject—animism [18]—which, like magic and taboo, is often considered a "period" in the development of religion; but here, again, the phenomena associated with animism belong to no especial age or people. Psychologists tell us that human beings in their development from childhood to maturity pass through the experience of the race in its upward growth. Thus a child will talk to a toy dog as if it were a living, sentient being; and if you were to protest that the dog did not understand what was said to it, the child would vigorously contradict you. He is passing through the animistic stage. I was amused recently by the facility with which a group of children became, in quick succession, tigers, lions, elephants, camels. They had been to the circus the day before.

This characteristic of the child is typical of the childhood of the race as well as of the savage of to-day. Each conceives of the things about him in terms of his own consciousness. The folk stories of all peoples abound in illustrations of this tendency. In one of the most graceful stories ever told, that of Cupid and Psyche, the mischievous Cupid falls in love with a mortal, Psyche, whose beauty, rivaling that of Venus, has won her divine honors. Venus, in hatred and jealousy, gains control of the unfortunate girl and imposes upon her several tasks which are quite impossible to execute without superhuman aid. One of these tasks is to fetch the golden fleece of certain sheep which browse along the banks of a near-by stream. Psyche, in desperation at her inability to perform the task, prepares to fling herself into the waters of the stream, when "rising from its flood, a green reed, nurse of sweet music, divinely inspired, thus prophesies, while a pleasant breeze sets it vibrating: 'Psyche, sorely tried by such great hardships as yours have been, pollute not my holy waters with your wretched, wretched death; approach not the dread sheep as long as they borrow their heat from the glow of the sun, when they are carried away, as is their wont, by a raging madness, when their

24

horns are sharp and their brows are stony, and, at times, their bites are poisonous and they are raging for the death of mortals. But until after midday has allayed the heat of the sun and the flocks have found rest in the serene river breeze, you can hide secretly beneath yonder tall plane tree which drinks the river waters just as I do. And as soon as the fury of the sheep is abated and they have relaxed their angry passions, cut through the foliage of the adjacent grove, and you will find the golden fleece clinging everywhere to the arched branches.' Thus prophesied the simple reed." [19]

E. B. Tylor, in his classic chapter on animism, [20] shows that primitive man believes that he possesses not only a body, but a shadowy image of his body, which in dreams and in trances can quickly flit from place to place, performing most of the actions of the real body. This belief is widespread even to-day among savages. Dreams, then, are a source of man's belief in spirits, and to the savage mind the experiences of the dream are as real as those of the waking moments. Frazer, for example, records [21] that an Indian had a dream in which his master compelled him to carry a canoe up several rapids. The next morning the Indian angrily reproved his master for assigning him such a hard task. He believed that his soul had left his body during the night. Hence it is that primitive peoples will not wake one who is sleeping, for if this is done suddenly, the spirit may not have time to return to the body. Carveth Wells, who spent six years among the Malays, writes: [22] "I never remember being actually called or awakened by a Malay servant. They consider it dangerous to waken a sleeping person because they believe that during sleep the body and soul are separated and that an attempt to awaken a person suddenly might result in instant death; so they wait patiently until their presence clse to a sleeper awakens him gradually."

Inasmuch, too, as the objects about him attended him on his journeys, primitive man assigned spirits to these. Again, shadows cast by his moving form, the echo of his voice from the hillside, his reflection in the lake—all tended to assist the spirit-making. Moreover, the observation that a corpse was different from a living body, especially in its lack of motion, led him to believe that something had disappeared from it—a spirit. In dreams the body was similarly inert, and thus he knew that in dreams the soul departed from it.

This wandering abroad of the soul in dreams finds expression in Lucretius: [23]

"Again, when sleep has bound the limbs in sweet repose and the whole body lies sunk in the deepest slumber, then, in spite of this, we are, as it seems to us, awake and moving our limbs. And in the inky darkness of the night we think we see the sun and the light of day; and, though in a confined place, we seem to be changing sky, sea, rivers, mountains, and to be crossing plains on foot, and to hear sounds, though everywhere the night is sternly silent; though in reality speechless, we seem to be speaking."

And again in Pliny the Elder [24] we read about the travels of a soul while the body was in a cataleptic state: the soul of Hermotimus of Clazomenae was wont to leave the body and to visit distant places, while the body, to all seeming, was lifeless. His enemies burned his body during one of these seizures and thus, as Pliny writes, "deprived the soul, on its return, of its sheath--if one may use that term."

In the animistic period, the things to which early man assigns spirits are those which help and those which oppose him in his struggle to survive: the cooling waters of the spring at which he slakes his thirst; the stream on which he launches his rude bark and from which he spears his fish for the support of life; the sky which sends cooling showers and causes his crops to grow, or parches them and brings blight and pestilence; the meteors which fall from heaven with a blaze of light, filling him with a strange awe; the fire which, in a friendly mood, parches his spelt and warms his body, but destroys his hut and his food when it is angry; the forest from whose twilight come wild beasts which mangle his sheep, or human enemies with whom he does battle to protect his wife and children. We might proceed almost ad infinitum enumerating the things to which the Roman gave spirits, so that Petronius and Pliny the Elder could correctly say that there were more spirits (numina) among the Romans than there were human beings. [25]

The animistic stage in the development of religion has been ascribed to the failure of magic. It would seem rather to be due to the growing self-consciousness of early man, resulting in a changed attitude toward the objects he wishes to influence. This shift in attitude may be seen by studying the manner in which early man, in the magic period, addresses the objects directly (naturalism) and, in the animistic period, the spirits resident in these objects. For an illustration of the former we shall draw upon Apuleius once more. [26] The witch Meroe plunges a sword up to the hilt into the neck of Socrates, catching the blood, as it gushes out, in a small bladder; and after thrusting her hand far into the entrails of his body, draws forth the heart. She then staunches the wound wlth a sponge, which she addresses as follows: "O sponge, born in the sea, beware lest thou pass over a running stream."

The transition stage between magic and animism is seen in Ovid's account of the Festival of Pales, where the farmer calls upon Pales "to appease the springs and the spirits of the springs." [27] Here, the farmer addresses first the springs (naturalism), then the spirits resident in them (animism).

We have already seen that in the magic stage the things which man, before experience with them, feels are potentially dangerous, he finds, after experience with them, are in some cases good (positive mana); and these he induces to help him by a magic act, assisted by an incantation or spell. The accompanying magic process is purely mechanical. The person performing the rite wills that a certain effect ensue, and this is bound to occur if the magic act and the incantation have been flawless. The volition lies with the person. The tendency of the growing mind of early man was to assign a spirit to the object addressed, and the incantation changed its character somewhat. But the difference between the spell of the period of magic and the prayer of the animistic period lies not so much in any inherent change in the nature of either, as in a shift in the attitude of mind toward the object to be influenced, and in the consequent alteration in the tone of the prayer. [28]

CHAPTER II
Positive and Negative Mana (Taboo)

AS SOON as man becomes self-conscious, he feels that anything different from himself is potentially, if not actually, dangerous: it contains a strange power to do him harm, and he must, if this be possible, force it to do him good. If experience teaches him that it can only do him harm, he must shun it, or, if this be impossible, he must rid himself of the evil effects of the contagion. We have given the name mana to this mysterious force, whether actually helpful or harmful or potentially so. Mana which has been found to be harmful we call negative mana; mana which has been found to be good is usually called simply mana; to this we have given the name positive mana. For example, with the growth of agriculture, rain is found necessary for the success of crops, and so a magic process, imitating the overflowing of the heavens, is performed to induce rain. This is rain in its positive or helpful aspect (positive mana). But rain sometimes has the power to harm (negative mana), and so the savage uses a magic act to avert rains which are flooding his fields.

Negative mana has been considered a form of negative magic. Just as in homoeopathic or in contagious magic (as we shall see in our chapter on magic acts) [1] man performs certain actions in accordance with the laws of similarity or contact that certain results may ensue, so, in accordance with the same principles, he will refrain from certain acts, or things, or persons, for fear that evil may result. It would be better, as we have suggested, to consider taboo as negative mana; for certainly all cases of taboo cannot be classified as negative magic. Positive and negative mana, then, are mysterious powers—good and evil—and magic (magic act and incantation) is the means used to secure the good and to avoid or ward off the evil.

Whatever the origin of taboo, the feeling in the mind of the person involved is that certain objects, actions, or persons are, for some reason unknown to him, possessed of a mysterious power which makes them dangerous. They should, therefore, be avoided. If, for some reason, contact is unavoidable, purificatory rites must be performed to wipe out the contagion—usually by the use of water. This involves magic action. There is scarcely a person, for example, unless he be a physician or an employee in an abattoir, who does not shrink from the sight of blood. Again, foreigners cause feelings of fear, as does a strange food, a new system of medicine, or a novel religious cult; but when one has eaten the strange food and found it palatable, when one has adopted the new system of medicine or the religious cult, the fears vanish.

The dread of danger inherent in things arises from several causes: it may, as some think, be instinctive, or it may arise from the savage's ignorance of the things which surround him in his struggle for existence. This ignorance may be due, as we have already indicated, to the fact that his brain is not developed enough physiologically for him to make proper associations and to come to right conclusions. Coupled with this is an unusually active imagination. From these ultimate causes spring certain specific causes of taboo:

the thing may be strange, or new, or abnormal, and hence dangerous. One may have had unpleasant associations with something which resembles the thing feared; the taboo may have been deliberately made by the priest or chieftain for selfish or even for social reasons; or the taboo may have arisen from trial and error, until the mana has been found to be positive or negative. However, taboo goes so far back into the dawn-twilight of the race and contains so many complex elements that it is difficult to explain every case satisfactorily.

Blood

We now return to the story of Torquatus with which we introduced our first chapter. Torquatus, it will be recalled, tore a bloody necklace from a Gaul whom he had killed in a hand-to-hand combat, and placed it, still reeking with blood, about his own neck. The feeling, vague and undefined though it was to the mind of the Roman, seems to be that, by wearing the Gaul's necklace about his own neck and by coming in contact with his blood, Torquatus might possess, in addition to his own personal strength, the strength of the Gaul.

A striking parallel to this incident is recorded in a much later day. The Emperor Commodus Antoninus often appeared before the people as a gladiator. According to the story, shortly before his death he plunged his hand into the wound of a slain gladiator and wiped the blood on his own forehead. He apparently had the feeling that he could thus, by contact with the blood of the gladiator, acquire from him bravery and skill, which he most certainly lacked, for the Roman people often snickered at his pretense of gladiatorial prowess. [2]

The interpretations of these actions may become clearer through a somewhat detailed study of the attitude of the Romans toward blood. But first let us examine the statements of two modern scholars on this subject. W. Warde Fowler writes thus about the taboo on blood among the Romans: [3] "... at Rome, so far as I can discover, there was in historical times hardly a trace left of this anxiety in its original form of taboo." Again, H. J. Rose says: [4] "... as the late W. Warde Fowler has repeatedly pointed out, the Romans had very little, if any, superstitious horror of blood."

That the Romans had little superstitious horror of blood seems a natural inference to make when we consider the fact that the Roman citizen was primarily a soldier, hardened to the shedding of blood on the battlefields, and that the blood of sacrifice at the altars and at the gladiatorial combats was an everyday sight. Despite this, a considerable body of evidence can be brought forward to show that the Romans did have an uncanny feeling about blood. Seneca, for example, writes: [5] "Some say that they themselves suspect that there is actually in blood a certain force potent to avert and repel a rain cloud." It was dangerous to have the blood of a living person over one's head. [6] Tibullus curses with these words a woman whom he hates: [7] "May she eat bloody food." The skeptical Ovid refuses to believe that mere water can wipe away bloodstains. [8] Some Romans believed that blood was the seat of the soul. [9] The ancient Hebrews also believed that the life resided in the blood. [10]

The dangerous character of blood is further suggested by the common accounts of rains of blood. [11] There is at least one reference to a rain of flesh. [12] Among the prodigies recorded during the Hannibalic War, we read that at Praeneste shields sweated blood, that the waters of Caere were mixed with blood, that both water and blood gushed from the springs of Hercules, and that bloody ears of wheat were garnered at Antium. [13] Again, later in the same war, reports reached Rome that statues sweated blood, and that again the waters of Caere were mixed with blood. [14] Tullia, the daughter of Servius Tullius, drove her carriage over the dead body of her father, and she was, in consequence, spattered with blood. Some of this blood accidentally contaminated her Penates and those of her husband. Soothsayers who were consulted predicted that, because of this bloodstain, the last of the Tarquins was doomed to suffer the same fate as Servius Tullius. [15] Once, while Flaminius was sacrificing, a calf broke away, spattering several spectators with its blood. This was considered terrible and ominous by the people present. [16] In 460 B.C., during the quarrels between the plebeians and the Senate, a large number of slaves and exiles seized the Capitol and the Citadel. After they had been driven out, the temple was purified, since many of them had desecrated it with their blood. [17] On one occasion, while the Emperor Caligula was sacrificing, he was spattered with the blood of a flamingo. Again, toward the end of the reign, during a performance of a broad farce, an actor, playing the part of a brigand, vomited blood. At the conclusion of the piece, a group of actors entertained the audience with such a vigorous burlesque of the brigand's vomiting that the stage overflowed with blood. These prodigies, among others, were believed to forebode the death of Caligula. [18] The Emperor Domitian abhorred blood; and once he proposed an edict that oxen should not be sacrificed. [19]

We recall the horror of Sallust in recounting the gruesome story that Catiline and his followers drank human blood to seal their covenant of crime. [20] A similar charge was made against the early Christians. Minucius Felix, the first of the Christian Latin writers, in his Octavius, a work written to defend his faith, writes (IX):

"What men say about the initiation of the novices is as abominable as it is well known. A baby, covered with spelt to deceive the unwary, is set before the person who is to be initiated into the sacred rites. The initiate, roused to inflict blows which, because of the covering of spelt, seem harmless, kills the child with hidden, secret stabs. Then—shocking to tell—they thirstily lick up the baby's blood and eagerly distribute its limbs. Through this victim they are linked in covenant; through complicity in the crime they are pledged to mutual silence."

This mystic association with blood finds curious expression in a story recorded [21] about the mutiny of the Roman soldiers under Germanicus. Later, realizing their crime, they felt that, by shedding the blood of the ringleaders, they might atone for their sins of rebellion. A bloody massacre took place in the camp. When Germanicus appeared on the scene, the soldiers repented but, still "seeing red," they wanted to cross the Rhine into Germany, again to atone with their blood for their murdered comrades. A Roman would vow vengeance by the bloodstained sword of a murderer. [22] A curious bit of military lore is recorded in Gellius. [23] According to the old military laws, when a soldier had committed an offense involving dishonor, a vein was opened, and the "bad blood" was let out. Gellius has suggested that the procedure may have been medicinal at first and may have been applied later to all soldiers for a variety of offenses. The reason goes deep into the past of the Romans. The blood contained the life principle of the man; and as he had shown by his actions that his life-blood was bad, it was drawn off to allow better life to enter his body.

It would seem that the earliest Roman sacrifices were bloodless. [24] Ceres was said to have been the first to receive animal sacrifice—the pig. [25] Only bloodless sacrifices might be made to Genius on birthdays, though it is probable that animal sacrifices were permitted on other days. [26] The first day of the Festival of Minerva had to be free from blood. [27] No animal sacrifice was made to Venus nor to Terminus on the Capitol. [28] Originally there was no animal sacrifice on the Festival of Pales; and the reason, as given by Plutarch [29] was that the festival might be free from bloodstains. Fowler remarks [30] the absence of the mention of blood in sacrifices, but he fails to recognize that this very absence is an indication that blood was taboo.

The Priest of Jupiter (Flamen Dialis) was not allowed to mention raw meat. [31] Plutarch suggests [32] that the repulsive appearance of meat and its likeness to the flesh of a wound may be the reason for the taboo. This uncanny aversion which the Romans felt for raw meat is further shown by a story told about the Emperor Maximus (238 A.D.). It seems that at the time of his birth an eagle dropped a large piece of beef into the house through the opening in the roof and that no one would touch it because of superstitious fear. [33] The Priest of Jupiter was forbidden also to pass under a vine which was trained on an arbor. [34] Frazer suggests a possible explanation of this taboo. [35] The juice of the grape was considered blood because it was red and looked like blood; and it was believed to contain the spirit. Moreover, wine was intoxicating, and so the soul of the vine could be felt actually at work in the person who drank the wine. There is another possible interpretation of the prohibition: the intertwining tendrils of the vine would make it dangerous to a priest. [36]

Ovid represents Numa performing sacrifice, before which he had to refrain from the pleasures of love and from flesh, and he might wear no ring. [37] A priest who had been splashed with the blood of a sacrificial animal was unclean until he had changed his dress. [38] We recall that AEneas could not touch his home-gods until he had cleansed the bloodstains from his hands with pure water. [39]

Blood, too, had a magic part in religious rites. We shall describe its use in three of these.

On October fifteenth, the Field of Mars witnessed a chariot race. The right-hand horse of the pair which won the race was killed, and blood from his tail was allowed to drip onto the sacred hearth. [40] This blood, together with the blood from his head, was mixed with sulphur and with bean straw, and with the ashes of unborn calves which had been sacrificed at the Festival of the Slaying of the Pregnant Cows (Fordicidia) on April fifteenth. The mixture was dispensed by the Vestals as a fertility charm at the Festival of Pales (Palilia) on April twenty-first. [41] Farmers and flocks at this festival leaped through bonfires into which some of the mixture had been thrown. It is not my plan to attempt, at this juncture, an explanation of these rites; for our purpose it is sufficient to note that in this rite blood had a peculiar magic property—probably the transmission of life, by sympathetic magic, from the prolific cow through the blood of her calves to the people who used the mixture.

Again at the Festival of the Lupercalia on February fifteenth blood from the sacrificial goats was smeared with a knife on the foreheads of two youths by some of the priests called Luperci, and then was wiped off with wool by other priests. [42] Much has been written in attempted explanation of this element in the rite. We shall return to the subject in a later chapter; here again we must be satisfied with pointing out merely the fact that blood was believed to possess some strange property.

Once more, at the Festival of Terminus, the god of boundaries, in the county districts at least, blood from the sacrificial victim, together with its bones and ashes, incense, and various products of the farm, was lowered into a hole in the ground and the boundary stone was rammed into it. [43] The worship of such stones was doubtless fetishism at first; but let us apply the rule for distinguishing a fetish from a god, as given by Dr. Jevons: [44] "If the object is the private property of some individual, it is fetish; if it is worshipped by the community as a whole, it, or rather the spirit which manifests itself therein, is a god of the community." The stone, in historical times, certainly was by this definition a god, or, to be more exact, a numen, worshiped by the farm community for the good of the farm. But it is hard to believe that the worship of such stones and of Terminus in the Capitol had developed far beyond the fetish stage.

The blood of foreigners, especially of enemies, was felt to be dangerous. The spear which the war-herald (fetial) threw into the enemy's country as a declaration of war was dipped in blood. [45]

The blood, being taboo from the point of view of the enemy, was calculated to do harm to him. The head of the spear might be of iron, which, as we shall presently find, had magic force. The soldiers who followed the general's triumphal car wore garlands of laurel, that they might enter the city with the stain of human blood removed. [46] A priest, known as the verbenarims, accompanied the war-heralds, carrying with him for purificatory purposes the sacred herbs, probably the modern vervain which is commonly believed to possess magic properties. [47]

On March nineteenth occurred the lustration of the sacred shields of the Leaping Priests of Mars (Salii), and probably of the whole army before it went forth to war. There was a procession in which these priests performed ceremonial dances, beating their shields and brandishing their spears—originally a magic ceremony to drive away malevolent spirits. Again, after the war season was over, the shields and, doubtless, the whole army were again lustrated and the shields were put away for the winter. [48] It has been suggested that the lustration in October was to disinfect both arms and men from the double stain of blood and of contact with foreign influences. [49] We meet with a similar ceremony at the conclusion of the war against Fidenae in the reign of Tullus Hostilius, when the king performed purificatory rites to rid the army of the taint of blood and of contact with the enemy. [50] All people at all times have believed that the spirits of the slain haunt their slayers. [51] The spirits of enemies killed in battle would naturally haunt the soldiers who slew them; hence the need of such purificatory rites for armies.

There is a curious story recorded in Tacitus [52] which seems to involve the taboo on blood. It appears that Arminius, the chief of the Cheruscans, in order to facilitate his escape from the Germans, "disfigured himself by smearing blood over his face." This, on the principle that "like cures like," would drive away blood and death from himself. Perhaps he smeared his face with blood so that the malevolent spirits of the men whom he had killed might be unable to recognize and haunt him. The practice of smearing the face and body with paint of clay (particularly if it is red) is common among savages. Prospective brides in the Congo region of Africa parade before the men who desire mates. These girls are covered with red clay, which is washed off in the river as soon as they are chosen as wives. [53]

Sufficient evidence has been presented thus far to show that the Romans, despite their putative indifference to blood because of the daily association with it on the battlefield and at the altars, did actually have a superstitious horror of blood. It was used in magic, and in religious rites with magic force. Blood was considered the seat of the soul of man; it was dangerous to have the blood of a living person over one's head; bloodstains were considered dangerous; prodigies involving blood were held to be especially ominous; blood was believed to have a mystic power to wipe out blood-guilt and to seal covenants of crime. If a soldier's actions were bad, his blood was believed to be bad, and hence it might be drawn off to allow good blood to take its place. The earliest sacrifices of the Romans were bloodless: even in some rites in historical times blood sacrifice was forbidden. In certain other rites, the blood of sacrifice was thought to possess magic properties. At least one priest was not allowed to mention flesh, much less touch it. The blood of foreigners was dangerous, and purificatory rites had to be performed to remove contagion. We shall presently see that the presence of blood at the birth of a child may also possibly account for the danger which was characteristic of that period.

How did the taboo on blood arise? According to some scholars the fear of blood is instinctive. A horse, for example, will shy at blood. Antiquity furnishes at least one example of this. [54] To our thinking, the taboo in many cases arose in some such way as this: when the savage shed his blood, suffered and died as the result of a wound, either accidental or from the blow of an enemy, his fellows associated the blood with the idea of pain and death—a familiar principle of similarity—and hence thereafter avoided blood.

Women

We know that women, under certain conditions, are considered dangerous by savage peoples. This may be due to the fact that they are physically weak or to the fact that they differ physiologically from men and, on that account, are potentially dangerous; or the taboo may be due to the superstitious horror of blood—particularly the blood of menstruation and of childbirth—common to all peoples.

The Laws of Moses say that a woman who had given birth to a boy was unclean for seven days; [55] if she gave birth to a girl, she was unclean for two weeks; [56] and she was not allowed to touch anything sacred or to enter the sanctuary until after that period. [57] Furthermore, if she had an issue of blood, she had to be put apart for seven days, and anyone who touched her was unclean until night. [58]

According to Pliny the Elder [59] a woman in her menstrual period will sour must, make grain barren, kill grafts, wither vegetables, dull mirrors, and do a host of other harmful things.

"During certain periods," writes Lafcadio Hearn [60] of Shinto worship in Japan, "women must not even pray before the miya, much less make offerings or touch the sacred vessels, or kindle the lights of the Kami."

A rather amusing incident involving the feeling of danger in the presence of women occurred recently. Sailors on board the American liner George Washington laid the buffeting which wintry storms inflicted upon their ship to the presence of a woman stowaway in the coal bunker. A woman, they said, had no place where men only were allowed. Her presence had caused all their woes during the voyage. [61]

The taboo on women was prevalent in Rome. At the country rites of Mars Silvanus no woman was allowed to be present or to see how the rites were performed. [62] Women were not allowed to swear by Hercules, and were forbidden to take part in his worship at the Greatest Altar in the Cattle Market. The story goes that Hercules, while driving through Italy the cattle which he had stolen in Spain from the three-headed monster Geryon, came upon women celebrating the rites of the Good Goddess and, being thirsty after the defeat of the fire-monster Cacus, he asked for a drink from their sacred spring. Now men were rigidly excluded from these rites, and so the women refused his request, for it would have been sacrilege for a man's lips to touch the spring. Hercules, in anger, burst open the door of the temple and drained the spring dry. In consequence of this refusal, he ordered that all women be excluded from his rites at the Greatest Altar which he erected in celebration of his victory over Cacus. [63] The tale, of course, was invented to explain the exclusion of women. Fowler has suggested [64] an explanation of the taboo, on the ground that the cult of Hercules had been superimposed on an older cult of Genius or the male principle. From this cult, quite naturally, women would be excluded. However, the presence of the Leaping Priests of Mars in the rites seems to suggest Mars, rather than Genius, behind the later Hercules. We know, too, that women were excluded from the worship of Hercules at Lanuvium. [65] Frazer retells [66] from Aelian a story which so humorously indicates the antipathy of Hercules for women that we shall introduce it at this point.

"Cocks were kept in the temple of Hercules [he writes] and hens in the temple of Hebe, and they had the run of a yard, in which, however, the plots assigned to the two sexes were strictly divided by a stream of pure running water. No hen ever presumed to trespass on the ground sacred to cocks and to Hercules; but whenever the cocks desired to mate they crossed the stream and coupled with the hens, and when they returned the running stream purified them from the pollution they had incurred by contact with the other sex."

Festus mentions the fact that in certain rites, undefined by him, women and girls were bidden to depart. [67] There has survived a law, traditionally attributed to Numa, to the effect that no kept mistress might touch the temple of Juno, and that if she did so, she must, with flowing hair, offer up an ewe lamb to the goddess. [68]

That the Romans early overcame their uneasiness about the presence of women in religious rites is shown by the fact that the

overseer's wife on a farm had certain minor religious duties to perform. [69] Again, the farmer's wife at the Festival of the Boundary Stone
brought fire from the home hearth for use on the altar erected at
the boundary of the farm. [70] On the day of the Liberalia, old women
crowned with ivy, called priestesses of Liber (sacerdotes Liberia),
made sacrificial cakes on portable hearths, which, with honey, were
bought and offered to Liber in the interest of the buyers. [71]

Children

One of the most arresting studies in the religious and superstitious
life of any people is the part played in it by the child. The fairest
festival of the Christian Church centers about the birth of a Child;
the most finished art of the Church has as its subject the Mother
and Child; much of the charm of the Christian ritual is due to the
presence of altar and choir boys. So, too, in ancient Rome, children
played an important part in many rites, both in the State religion and
in rites which were performed in secret, outside the pale of religion.

It will be our purpose to study, somewhat in detail, the part
played by children in the superstitious and in the religious life of the
Romans. We shall have something to say about their place
(1) in witchcraft, and more especially in murder rites of witches;
(2) in prehistoric rites of child sacrifice;
(3) in divination, both inside and outside the recognized religion;
(4) in connection with taboos and superstitions;
(5) in religious rites, (a) at birth, (b) at puberty, and (c) at death; then

(6) we shall indicate some of their functions as acolytes in the home and in the fully developed State religion; and, finally,

(7) we shall seek to explain, somewhat more fully than has hitherto been done, the reasons for the place of the child in witchcraft and in religion.

1. THE CHILD IN WITCHCRAFT

It is a well-known fact that Roman parents would consult astrologers in order to learn the future of their children. Then, too, as we shall see, women regularly worshiped divinities whose special province was assistance at childbirth and prophecy concerning children. Credulous mothers, would often consult witches about these matters.

It was probably the mother of Horace who first introduced him to witchcraft by taking him to a local witch in order to secure foreknowledge of her son's career. At least this is suggested in a childhood reminiscence of his association with witches, in the well-known passage which constitutes a part of Horace's famous description of his encounter with the bore in the Sacred Road. [72] Though the story is doubtless fanciful-told to heighten the effect of the satire—it is probably based on fact and shows that fortune-telling by witches was prevalent in the country districts. Horace, we recall, when vainly trying to rid himself of the bore, asks the latter if he has any relatives who are interested in his welfare; if the bore answers "Yes," Horace will tell him that he is on his way to visit a sick friend who has a contagious disease. The bore, however, answers: "I have no one. I have laid them all to rest." "Happy they!" replies Horace.

"Now I remain. Finish me. For the sad fate is pressing close upon me which a Sabellian hag, having shaken her holy urn, once prophesied to me when I was a boy. 'Him neither dire poison nor hostile blade will carry off, nor pleurisy, nor cough, nor crippling gout. A garrulous fellow will sometime do him to death. If he be wise, let him avoid the talkative when once he has grown to manhood.'"

The Romans commonly believed that witches murdered children to secure parts of their bodies for use in their gruesome rites. Horace [73] gives us a picture of certain witches murdering a boy to use his entrails in plying their art. The poem opens with the cries of the boy, who is being spirited away from his home by four witches. One of them, Canidia, orders wild fig trees to be uprooted from the tombs, the eggs and down of a screech owl to be smeared with toad's blood, and poisonous grasses and bones snatched from the maw of a hungry bitch to be consumed in magic flames. Sagana sprinkles the house with waters from Lake Avernus, and Veia, with her hoe, digs up the earth to bury the boy with only his head protruding, that he may die there of starvation in the sight of food changed again and again during the day. Canidia, as she gnaws her long nails, prays to Night and to Diana that the charms which she has already used may work on her aged lover, Varus. But some other witch has worked a stronger counter-charm: so Canidia, too, will prepare another. The poem closes with a curse from the boy who cries that he will, as an avenging spirit, hound the witches.

Witches would steal babies for use in their rites and would leave bundles of straw in their place. We have an illustration of this practice in Petronius. [74] Trimalchio relates that when he was a boy, the favorite of his master, a mere child, died; and while the boy's mother was bemoaning his death, witches were heard screeching outside. A husky Cappadocian, one of Trimalchio's household, rushed out to slay them, returning, however, black and blue from the encounter. He later died—a raving maniac. The mother, on returning to her child, found merely a bundle of straw. The witches had carried off the dead child for use in their nefarious business.

Witches, probably midwives in some cases, occasionally removed unborn children by unnatural means from their mothers' wombs and placed them on magic altars. [75] The entrails, urine, caul, teeth, liver, marrow and other parts of boys were used in these rites. The caul of a child, for instance, was often seized by midwives and sold to superstitious lawyers, for it was believed to have the power to bring them luck while pleading. [76] It is not difficult to credit this when we recall that Regulus, a lawyer contemporary with Pliny the Younger, would daub paint around his right eye if he was to plead for a plaintiff and around the left eye if for a defendant, and would transfer a white adhesive plaster from one eyebrow to the other, depending on the nature of the case which he was pleading. [77]

Not only were professional witches and wizards accused of murdering children for magic purposes, but sometimes men in public life were also charged with these practices. Cicero, for example, in a speech attacking Vatinius, a political adventurer and henchman of Julius Caesar, charged him, among other things, with using the vitals of a boy in questionable rites. [78] Justin Martyr in a much later day accused the Romans of practicing divination from murdered children. [79] Such heinous crimes were in later times committed even in the emperor's palace. One of the horrible deeds of Heliogabalus, recorded by AElius Lampridius, was that he sacrificed beautiful children of noble birth whose parents were still living. For this purpose he kept magicians in his household; and he himself would torture his victims and examine their vitals. [80]

2. CHILD SACRIFICE

It may be possible that the murder of children in witchcraft was a survival from a period when children were actually sacrificed in accordance with the rites of accepted religion. With the growing revulsion of feeling against taking human life, substitutes were offered in place of the child victims in recognized religious rites, while murder itself was relegated to the darkness of forbidden witchcraft. Be that as it may, there is a gruesome suggestion of human sacrifice in the tradition that boys were sacrificed to Mania, the mother of the Lares, at the Festival of the Cross-Roads (Compitalia)—an offering calculated to guarantee the welfare of families. At the expulsion of the Tarquins, the custom was abolished by Brutus, who ordered that heads of garlic and poppies be sacrificed in place of boys. [81]

3. CHILDREN IN DIVINATION

The ancients commonly used boys in rites of divination both privately in magic and in forms sanctioned by the State. Thus, one of the charges brought against Apuleius of Madaura in Africa, in the famous trial under the proconsul Claudius Maximus of Sabrata, was that he used a boy in certain magic rites. [82] According to the charge, he spirited a boy away to a secret spot and there, in the presence of a few witnesses, at an altar under the flickering light of a lantern, performed magic rites, after which the boy collapsed, falling to the ground—as his enemies declared, bewitched, but, according to Apuleius, in a fit of epilepsy. On regaining consciousness, he was found to be out of his mind. That boys were thus used in magic rites for divination and prophecy Apuleius asserts on the authority of Varro who, he says, tells how at Tralles a boy was used to determine the probable outcome of the Mithridatic War. The boy gazed into a vessel of water at an image of Mercury there reflected and proclaimed his prophecy in verse. Apuleius relates also that Fabius, after losing a large sum of money, had consulted Nigidius who, by means of incantations, so bewitched certain boys that they were able to reveal the spot where a part of the money was concealed. The remainder had been dissipated, and one coin had come into the hands of Marcus Cato the Philosopher, who, on being questioned, acknowledged possession of it. Apuleius apparently credits such prophecies and believes that the human soul, especially when it is young and innocent, can, by means of music and sweet perfumes, be lulled to sleep—hypnotized—and in that state can predict what will happen in the future. Boys who perform such functions must be beautiful, without physical blemish, quick-witted and ready of speech. We may compare, in this respect, the requirements for the girls who presented themselves as priestesses of Vesta. [83] They must, among other things, be free from impediments in speech, must possess good hearing and must, like animals offered in sacrifices to the gods, have no bodily defect.

An interesting instance of unconscious divination by a child is recorded in Cicero's treatise On Divination. [84] When Lucius AEmilius Paulus, having been chosen to wage war against Perseus, King of Macedonia, returned home, he noticed that his daughter was sad. On inquiry, he found that her pet puppy Persa had died. The father—he had been an augur—took this as a prophecy that King Perseus was doomed to death. It is not difficult to believe that this incident actually happened; but it takes a stretch of the imagination to credit the story recorded by Livy [85] that in the fifth year of the Second Punic War a baby called out from its mother's womb, "Io Triumphe!"

The Emperor Didius Julianus, assisted by magicians, performed certain rites in which boys, with bandages over their eyes, gazed, as it seemed, into a mirror while charms were muttered over their heads. While in this state one of the boys declared that he saw in the mirror the coming of Severus as emperor and the departure of Julianus. [86]

4. SUPERSTITIONS CONCERNING CHILDREN
– TABOO

Many superstitions concerning children at birth have been preserved for us in Roman writers. Thus both the new-born child and its mother are considered uncannily dangerous. This may be due to their physical weakness and to the presence of blood at birth. [87] It is for fear that the weakness of the child may bring a corresponding weakness to the father that an English gypsy father to-day will not touch his child until it is several months old. [88] It was for the same reason, perhaps, that a Gallic father, in Caesar's day, would not allow his son to come into his presence until he had grown up and could endure military service. [89] The feeling that mother and child were surrounded by evil forces survived among the Romans of historical times. It was natural, then, that they should seek means not only to shield the child from evil influences but to protect those who came in contact with it as well.

The danger surrounding the mother and her child is well illustrated in the superstition that they were liable to be tormented by evil spirits from the woodland—Silvanus, as the later Romans believed—until a curious ceremony was performed. I quote St. Augustine: [90]

"... After the birth of the child, three protecting divinities are summoned lest the god Silvanus enter during the night and harass mother and child; and to give tokens of those guardian divinities three men by night surround the threshold of the house and first strike it with an ax and a pestle; then they sweep it off with a broom, that, by giving these signs of worship, the god Silvanus may be kept from entering. For trees are not cut nor pruned without iron; nor is spelt powdered without a pestle; nor is grain piled up without a broom. Now from these three objects are named three divinities: Intercidona from the intercisio of the ax; Pilumnus from the pilum; Deverra from the sweeping (verrere) of the broom; and by the protection of these divinities new-born babies are preserved against the violence of Silvanus."

The objects used in this rite are charms against evil influences: the iron of the ax and the iron tip of the pestle are familiar objects for averting evils. The ceremonial sweeping drives away evils from the child.

The Roman child up to the age of puberty needed the protection of a special purple-bordered dress which has been shown to have possessed religious significance. [91] Again, boys and girls wore about their necks amulets of gold or of skin, usually containing a representation of the phallus, but occasionally a green lizard or a heart and perhaps also other objects. These were believed to ward off baleful influences, especially the evil eye. When the child doffed his boyish dress, he hung up his amulet on the Lares. [92]

Children were liable to be harassed by bloodsucking vampires in the form of owls. The rites of riddance, described by Ovid [93] in the case of the infant Procas, are as follows:

"Immediately she (Crane) touches the doorposts three times in succession with a spray of arbutus; three times she marks the threshold with arbutus spray. She sprinkles the entrance with water (and the water contained a drug). She holds the bloody entrails of a pig, two months old, and thus speaks: 'Birds of the night, spare the entrails of the boy. For a small boy a small victim falls. Take heart for heart, I pray, entrails for entrails. This life we give you in place of a better one.'"

Having killed the sow, the witch placed the vital organs in the open air and forbade those attending the rite to look upon them. Then a whitethorn branch was set in a small window which furnished light for the house. After that the child was safe and the color returned to his pallid face.

The principle of similarity in this magic act is evident: the vital organs of the child which, in early Roman times, were under the care of the goddess Carna, are to be saved by the vicarious offering of the vitals of a sow. The pig was frequently so used. A similar substitution is to be seen in the ceremony of treaty-making, preserved by Livy. [94]

The child, too, was liable to be harmed by the evil eye. Persius satirizes the old woman—an adept at averting the evil eye—who takes a baby from its cradle and applies spittle to its forehead and lips with the middle finger. [95] The goddess of the cradle (Cunina) was believed, in popular superstition at least, to have the power of averting the evil eye. [96]

Several superstitions with regard to the luckiness or unluckiness of children at birth are recorded by Pliny the Elder. Thus, inasmuch as it was contrary to nature for a baby to come into the world foot-foremost, such a birth was considered unlucky. [97] The child who at birth had caused the death of its mother was believed to have been born under happy auspices. [98] For a girl to be born with teeth was considered ominous. [99] It would seem that the birth of triplets caused parents no uneasiness, but that when four children were born it was considered ill-omened. [100] So when, in the principate of Augustus, a certain woman of low origin gave birth to two boys and two girls, it was believed to presage a famine which took place shortly afterward. [101]

Savages believe that blood and anything that looks like blood has the power to drive away evils. A survival of this superstition may account for the custom which obtained in the family of the Emperor Albinus (196 A.D.), requiring that new-born children be wrapped in bandages of a reddish color. [102]

The Romans, in common with many other peoples, ancient and modern, often identified the lifetime of a particular tree with the duration of the life of the person at whose birth it was planted.

So on the country estate of the Flavians stood an ancient oak which sent forth a branch on each of three occasions when Vespasia gave birth to a child. [103]

5. THE CHILD IN RELIGIOUS RITES
a. At Birth

Tertullian [104] acquaints us with a whole series of divinities which looked after the interests of the child before and after birth. Among these Fluviona cared for the child in its mother's womb; Candelifera was the spirit of the light—equivalent magically to the life of the child—which was placed in the room where the baby was born; Cunina, in addition to having the power of averting the evil eye, supplied quiet; Levana presided over the ceremonial lifting of the child from the ground by the father. It has been suggested [105] that the new-born baby was placed on the ground that it might receive a soul from Mother Earth; for among savages even to-day the belief prevails that babies at birth are not possessed of souls.

Ovid [106] distinguishes two goddesses of birth, Postverta and Porrima, the former for children born foot-first, the abnormal posture, and the latter for the child born normally. Other names for Porrima were Prorsa and Antevorta. In all likelihood they were names of two carmentes. We know that the names Porrima and Postverta were mumbled by the priests. This explains the uncertainty of the names of the divinities and leads one to suspect that they originated in magic. And indeed the worship of the Roman Carmenta (Carmentis) may have originated in magic; for, in old Latin, prophetesses were called carmentes and the scribes who copied out their prophecies were called carmentarii. These carmentes, as W. Warde Fowler has pointed out, [107] may well have been wise women whom prospective mothers consulted. But it is more likely that Carmenta was an old Italian divinity. In her rites, leather, except perhaps for the skins of the sacrificial animals, was taboo. The reason for this, as Ovid rightly indicates, [108] was to prevent the contagion of the dead animal from communicating death to the mother or to her child.

The goddesses most commonly invoked by mothers at the time of parturition were Juno Lucina, Diana, and Mater Matuta. These divinities seem to have displaced the carmentes in historical times. [109]

Springs were commonly worshiped by expectant mothers. Such a spring was that of Egeria in the sacred grove not far from the Capene Gate on the Appian Road. [110] Certain springs at Sinuessa were believed to possess, among other powers, that of preventing childlessness. [111]

The Romans, as we have seen, sought, by means of magic rites, to shield their children from evil influences. It was for this reason, doubtless, that the child was purified and given a name in accordance with religious forms—the boy on the ninth and the girl on the eighth day after birth. A goddess Nundina, it would seem, presided over the rites of purification. [112]

b. At Puberty

Another dangerous period in the life of the child was that of Puberty. At that period—usually on the day of the Festival of Liber (Liberalia)—the boy ceremonially put on the white dress of manhood (toga virilis) and laid aside, in the presence of the Lares, his amulet (bulla) and his magic boyhood dress. [113] This ceremony may have descended from a prehistoric rite of initiation of the lad into the clan. [114] According to the unknown author of a work De Praenominibus, the boy received a name on this day. If this be true, the child probably discarded the name which had been given to him on the dies lustricus. [115] I suggest that if the name given to him in infancy had proved magically lucky, he retained it; but if he had suffered disease, accident, or other misfortune, the name was changed at his "coming of age" ceremony.

c. At Death
The Romans both buried and burned their dead; but archaeologists have shown that the largest numbers of Roman burials were those of children—a fact which suggests that some superstition prohibited their cremation. [116] This archaeological evidence corroborates a statement in Pliny the Elder that it was not the custom to cremate children whose teeth had not yet appeared. [117]

6. THE CHILD AS ACOLYTE
Children, among all peoples, have definite roles assigned to them in religion, often in connection with rites of purification and of divination. For instance, according to an early Christian writer, Barnabas, [118] it would appear that in the popular religion of the Jews the most wicked men of their number would slay and burn a heifer. Boys would take the ashes and place them in vessels, and, with a stick bound with purple wool and hyssop, would sprinkle the people severally to cleanse them of their sins. As there is no mention of this

rite in the Old Testament, it is reasonable to suppose that it belonged to the popular religion.

The employment of children as acolytes in Roman religion originated in the primitive home where children alone, because of their purity, were allowed to handle the food in the storeroom. [119] After the first course of the meal had been removed, silence was enjoined, and an offering made on the hearth. Then the son of the family, according to the custom, announced whether the omens were favorable. [120] In certain rites in the fields, too, both boys and girls acted as assistants. At the Festival of Terminus in February each member of the family took part: the boy carried the basket containing products of the farm, which he threw into the fire on the altar; his sister offered honey cakes. [121]

Hence the Romans, because of childhood associations, often grew up with great affection for the gods of the home. Tibullus, for instance, describes [122] how he used to run as a child about the feet of the Lares, protected by their kindly influence.

Boys and girls called camilli and camillae, wearing the toga praetexta, often took part in Roman State rites. [123] They had to be free-born and both of their parents must be living. Hence the names patrimi and matrimi were also given to them. Three such boys took part in the procession which escorted the bride to her new home. One carried the whitethorn torch in front of the procession and the other two held the hands of the bride. [124] Even in our day in far separated parts of the world boys and girls take part in magic and religious rites, and both their parents must be living. [125]

At the request of the Emperor Augustus, Horace composed the

"Secular Hymn" [126] which was sung on the third day of the religious festival of 17 A.D., first at the temple of Apollo, then at the Capitol, by a chorus of twenty-seven boys and a like number of girls, whose parents were living. It seems that the Sibylline oracles had commanded that the boys and girls sing a hymn to the Roman divinities; and we suspect that the oracles were inspired by Augustus.

To summarize: We have seen that credulous Roman mothers would consult witches to secure assistance in childbirth and to learn the future of their children. The Romans commonly believed that witches murdered children—especially boys—to obtain parts of their bodies for use in their art; and that they would steal children for this purpose, leaving bundles of straw in their place. Occasionally, witches removed unborn children by unnatural means from their mothers' wombs. The vitals, urine, caul, teeth, liver and other parts of boys were used in their rites. The cauls of children were sold by mothers to superstitious lawyers, because they were believed to bring them luck in pleading. Persons in public life were occasionally charged with murdering children for questionable ends.

The murder of children in witchcraft may be a survival of actual child sacrifice in regular religious rites. In religion, substitutes were sacrificed in place of the children in historical times, and actual child murder was driven to cover in witchcraft.

Children were employed in divination both in the State religion and in private rites. Sometimes boys prophesied by gazing into water or into mirrors; sometimes under the influence of hypnosis. Such boys had to be physically perfect, intelligent, and ready of speech.

Occasionally, accidental events involving children were believed to have the force of divination.

The new-born baby and its mother were considered magically dangerous, and rites had to be performed to protect them and anyone who came in contact with them. They were, for example, liable to be harassed by evil spirits from the woodland, and a set ceremony was prescribed to remove these evils. Children, too, might be tormented by vampires, and rites of riddance were performed to dispel these. Up to the age of puberty, the child was protected by a magic dress, and by an amulet which contained objects calculated to ward off the evil eye. These were discarded when he came of age.

The position and condition of the child at birth had much to do with his subsequent luckiness or unluckiness.

The Romans, like so many other peoples, believed that the life of a person was dependent on the duration of the life of a tree which had been planted at his birth.

Numerous divinities presided over the child from the time of conception to puberty. There was a divinity to care for his every action. Carmentes—originally prophesying witches—were also consulted by mothers. Women worshiped springs which, as they believed, assisted in parturition and prevented childlessness.

The name of the child had magic import; if it was found to be an unlucky one, it might be changed at puberty when children, at the Festival of Liber, doffed their magic dress and their amulets.

It seems that children who died in infancy, especially if they were still toothless, were buried, not cremated as was the case with adults.

In regular religious rites children were employed as acolytes. This originated in the primitive home where none but children were allowed to touch the sacred stores. The son announced omens in the home, and both boys and girls took part in State rites. Such children must be of free-born parents who were both living. Boys took part in wedding processions.

It is interesting to seek an explanation for the fact that children at certain times were considered magically dangerous, and for their use in religious rites. The presence of blood at birth was sufficient to make the child dangerous at that time. Again, the helplessness of the child made it possible for stronger forces of evil—vampires, the evil eye, and the like—to get control of him. On the other hand, the weakness of the child might have a dangerous influence on others, particularly on the father. Children were used in rites of divination because there was no possibility of their being influenced by experience. In rites where hypnosis was employed, their greater susceptibility to suggestion made them valuable agents. In religious rites, as we have seen, only the children of parents who were free-born and still living were employed. If the parents were not living, the loss in magic strength which the child suffered would be communicated to the religious rite, to say nothing of the evil effect of contact with death. That the child must be physically perfect is to be explained in the same way as the requirement that animals in sacrifice be unblemished: the defects of the child would be communicated magically to the rites. Again, sexual intercourse tends to weaken the effect of religious rites. Hence the effectiveness of children, who were still innocent and naive, for the performance of these rites.

Death and Corpses

In all ages, corpses have been looked upon as uncanny and as needing purificatory rites. "Primitive thought," writes Crawley, [127] "has no definition of the nature of death, but the usual attitude toward it, as may be inferred from mourning customs, is a mystic terror." Thus, among the uneducated Japanese of modern times, a corpse is felt to be dangerous, and precautions must be taken against infection. "One must not sleep, for example," says Lafcadio Hearn, [128] "or even lie down to rest, with his feet turned toward it. One must not pray before it, or even stand before it, while in a state of religious impurity,—such as that entailed by having touched a corpse, or attended a Buddhist funeral, or even during the period of mourning for kindred buried according to the Buddhist rite." The same feeling of danger arising from contact with death or corpses was common among the ancient Hebrews. For instance, any person who had been defiled by contact with the dead was debarred from the camp. [129] The person who had touched a dead body, the bones of a man, or a grave was unclean for seven days. [130]

We turn again to Rome. We have seen that witches, to effect their secret ends, would cut off parts of a dead body. [131] Cemeteries, then, would be their favorite haunt. Horace describes [132] the magic rites of four witches, by which one of them hopes to win back the affection of an aged lover. A boy is captured. He is buried up to the neck in the ground, in the heart of the witch's house, and there left to die of starvation. The object of this murder is to secure the marrow and liver, which are to be cut out and dried for use in a love potion. Unfortunately, there is reason to suspect that witches actually committed such gruesome crimes in Rome. But is it so strange that witch-murders occurred in ancient times, when to-day, in our own country, one may read about similar murders for magic purposes? [133]

It was believed that one's strength could be impaired by treading on a corpse. [134] A boy who had been performing acrobatic stunts on a ladder for the amusement of the guests at Trimalchio's dinner slipped and fell. Uproar ensued—not, as Petronius assures us, [135] because the boy had fallen, but because his death, especially since he was a slave, would have been ill-omened. Scipio Africanus the Elder was found one morning dead in bed. No inquest was made, [136] and we may readily believe that this omission was due to superstitious horror of the corpse. The Romans once refused to hazard battle because they discovered that the mound from which their general had addressed them was a burial place. [137] In 509 B.C., the dedication of the temple of Jupiter on the Capitol fell by lot to one of the consuls, Horatius. The friends of the other consul jealously tried to hinder the dedication. They concocted a scheme which, they thought, would play on Horatius' fear of contagion from death. When Horatius was already holding the door-post, praying to the gods, his enemies interrupted the rites, announcing "that his son was dead, and that he could not dedicate a temple when his household was thus tainted with death. [138] The consul, however, proceeded with the ceremony.

In 459 B.C. the regular five-year expiatory sacrifice at Rome was not held, because the Capitol had been stained with the blood of exiles and slaves and because a consul had been slain. [139] Germanicus, having arrived at the spot beyond the Rhine where the Roman general Varus and his legions had been annihilated by the Germans, helped with his own hands in the burial of his country's soldiers of an earlier day. The Emperor Tiberius, however, misinterpreted his actions, thinking "that a general, invested with the office of augur and other ancient religious functions, ought not to have assisted at the performance of funeral rites." [140]

A day was regularly set by the Roman consul for the enrollment of raw recruits in the army. The soldier was bound by oath to appear, unless prevented by specified reasons: among them the necessity of his presence at a funeral in his family, or at a rite of purification from contact with the dead. [141] Those who attended a Roman funeral procession, "on returning, were sprinkled with water and walked over fire...." [142] After a dead body had been taken out of a Roman house, a ceremonial sweeping of the house took place, performed probably by the heir, but possibly, as Ovid intimates, [143] by an officer, an assistant of the Priest of Jupiter.

Frazer furnishes a parallel to this custom. He writes: [144] " ... in Thuringia three heaps of salt are placed on the floor of a house in which a person has died; the room is then swept out, and the sweepings and the broom are carried to the churchyard or to the field; sometimes the mattress is burned in the field. The reason assigned for all these customs is to prevent the ghost from returning." The ceremonial sweeping in such rites is to brush the ghost of the dead man out of the house. Salt was regularly used in purifying rites among all peoples; and salt and spelt are also regular offerings to the souls of the dead. [145]

The boy who carried the whitethorn torch in the wedding

procession to the house of the bridegroom had to be the child of parents who were still living. [146] This requirement also applied to boys who sang in the chorus at the Secular Games. [147] The taboo on death doubtless caused this restriction; for if the parents were dead, the boys might have adversely affected the rites. The Priest of Jupiter was not allowed to set foot on a grave or touch a dead body. [148] It was the custom of the Romans to place a cypress before the house where a person had died, that the Chief Priest (Pontifex Maximus) might avoid contamination by shunning it. [149]

Not only were corpses considered dangerous, but so also were days on which the Romans celebrated the Festival of the Dead, when temples were closed, the altars were cold, and it was unpropitious for girls to marry. [150] The Laws of the Twelve Tables forbade the cremation or burial of a dead body within the city walls. [151] A law passed in 260 B.C. forbade burials in the city of Rome. Victorious generals and Vestals, however, were exempt from this prohibition. [152]

The nearest equivalent, perhaps, to the word taboo in Latin is religio; and it seems that the Romans at times used this word in the sense of taboo on death. [153] Varro, for instance, uses the term religiosa, with this connotation, of certain personal belongings of King Numa which, according to tradition, were believed to have been placed after his death in jars at a spot near the Cloaca Maxima in Rome. [154]

The origin of the feeling with regard to the dead seems to lie in man's instinct for self-preservation. We may give as an additional reason one of the principles of negative mana—that, among all peoples, things which are strange are to be avoided. Man must certainly at a very early time have noticed the agonies which his fellows suffered when mangled by wild beasts or pierced by the spear of the enemy. These agonies were accompanied by the shedding of blood, which was in itself felt to be dangerous. Furthermore, there was an observable cessation of all the man's normal actions. Hence early man associated pain, blood, and the cessation of action with the strange dead body and avoided it.

Curiously enough, the Romans, who deified almost everything, had no god of Death.

Leather

Leather, unless it were the skin of a sacrificial animal, was often considered dangerous by ancient peoples. Thus leather was prohibited in the worship of Carmentis, a goddess popular with prospective mothers; and the reason for this prohibition was, according to Ovid, [155] the fear that it might pollute the pure altars of the goddess. A woman would naturally fear that any part of a dead animal might cause death to the child or to herself. The taboo on leather seems to have applied also in other rites. [156] The wife of the Priest of Jupiter (Flaminica Dialis) might wear shoes or sandals made only of the skin of the sacrificial animal, or of an animal that had not met death naturally; for animals that had died natural deaths were considered unlucky. [157] The Jews were forbidden to eat a beast which had died a natural death: [158] "And if any beast, of which ye eat, die; he that toucheth the carcass thereof shall be unclean until the even."

At the Lupercalia the youthful priests wore skins of the sacrificial animals about their loins and used lashes made of them. They were otherwise naked. [159] We have seen that in the ceremony of rain-making women walked barefoot. [160] According to the testimony of Ovid women were also barefoot at the worship of Vesta. [161] The taboo in these cases may be ascribed both to the fear of knots and of things which bind and to the fear of leather.

The taboo on leather is certainly related to the taboo on corpses and death. A dead animal's skin would be dangerous to a sacred rite; and this would be particularly true (to repeat) if the animal had died a natural death. Hence the use of the skin of the sacrificial animal in religious rites. Since sandals were made of leather and were bound with thongs, the wearing of these would be forbidden, for the additional reason that they would bind up the rites as they bound up the feet—a principle which we shall note in our treatment of the taboo on knots.

Days

The days following the Kalends, the Nones, and the Ides of every month were called black days (dies atri) by the Romans. On these days no battle might be fought, no sacrifice made, no business, public or private, undertaken. [162] Occasionally, however, the taboo on sacrifice was waived, as, for example, after the defeat of the Romans at Lake Trasimenus when Hannibal threatened Rome. [163]

The Romans themselves explained black days as instituted

by a decree of the pontiffs in 389 B.C., made because on these days they had suffered severe reverses in battle—notably on the eighteenth of July when over three hundred members of the Fabian family were defeated at Cremera (477 B.C.) by the people of Veii, and at the Trebia where Hannibal was victorious over the Romans (217 B.C.). The generals in both cases had taken the omens and followed them with disastrous results; hence the prohibition of sacrifices on that day in later times.

The taboo on these days, if the historical explanation is correct—as well it may be—was artificial and not truly primitive. However, there is a possible explanation in another direction. [164] The Hindoos call the days when the moon is waning the "dark half" of the month, and when it is waxing they call it the "bright half." Now in Latin the word quinquatrus, the fifth day after the period when the moon is full and at its brightest—the Ides—may possibly be a compound of quinque and ater, thus making it the fifth of the black days when the moon is waning. By this etymology, the Tusculan terms triatrus, sexatrus, septematrus, and the Falernian decimatrus would be respectively the third, sixth, seventh, and tenth black days after the Ides, when the moon was on the wane. When the original meaning of the "black day"—that is, referring to the darkness of the moon—had been forgotten, the popular mind interpreted ater as meaning unlucky or tabooed.

The twenty-fourth of August, the fifth of October and the eighth of November were termed dies religiosi. On these days the spirits of the dead (manes) were believed to issue forth into the upper world through the mundus—the name given to a trench or entrance to a vault in the city of Romulus which was believed to be the gate of hell. [165] On these days, again, no public business might be undertaken, no battle fought, no army conscripted. This taboo is ascribable to the taboo on death and corpses. So, too, the taboo on death accounts for the fact that the days of the Parentalia in February and those of the Lemuria in May were religiosi. On the days in February known collectively as the Parentalia no temple might be open, no fire might burn on the altars, and no marriages could be performed. The magistrates laid aside their official dress for the day and wore that of ordinary citizens. [166]

June seventh, when the temple of Vesta was allowed to remain open, was religiosus. Fowler ascribes [167] the taboo on the day to "... some mystical purification or disinfection preparatory to the ingathering of the crops." It was considered unlucky for a Roman girl to marry on the Kalends, the Nones, or the Ides of any month. The pontiffs had decreed them "black" because, whenever on these days Roman generals petitioned the gods for success in battle, disasters followed. [168]

CHAPTER III
Miscellaneous Taboos

IN THE last chapter, after illustrating the terms positive and negative mana, we discussed the taboo on blood and five other taboos which are allied with it—on women, children, death, leather, and days. The present chapter will illustrate rather fully and attempt to explain several more taboos which were prevalent among the Romans—those on sex, men, strangers, slaves, and on linen, knots, iron and places.

Sex

Among all peoples, chastity is often obligatory before the performance of religious duties. In certain Roman priesthoods, the taboo on sexual intercourse lasted for a long period of years; in some religious rites, abstinence was enjoined only at specific times, particularly on the eve of a religious festival. Even outside the Roman State religion, chastity was occasionally required before the performance of certain daily tasks. The most familiar example of forced chastity over a period of years is that of the Vestal Virgins. Chastity as a preparation for religious rites was familiar at the festivals of Ceres and of Bacchus, both divinities of the products of the earth; we know, too, that beekeepers, on the day before they handled the hives, had to refrain from intercourse. [1]

The Vestal's vow of virginity lasted for thirty years. [2] During the first ten years she was a novice, during the next ten she performed the sacred duties of the order, and during the last ten she taught the girls who had just entered the order. After thirty years she was allowed to return to secular life and marry, if she chose, but this rarely happened.

One is forced to believe that the Vestals, despite their vows of chastity and their putative holiness, were a little lower than the angels. The maiden Tarpeia, who treacherously opened the portals of the Citadel to Tatius the Sabine, was a Vestal; she used her sacred office of drawing water from the holy spring of the Muses as a pretext for admitting the enemy. [3] If we are to give credence to these stories, unchastity among the Vestals seems to have been common. The founder of Rome saw the light of day as the result of the ravishing of the Vestal Rhea by the god Mars. In 483 B.C., soothsayers were consulted about the meaning of certain portents from the gods: they reported that sacred rites had been neglected. Accordingly, Oppia, a Vestal, was charged with having broken her vow, and was buried alive. [4] During the period of the First Samnite War, Minucia, a Vestal, brought suspicion upon herself because of her fondness for prety dresses; on the evidence of a slave she was charged with unchastity and was buried alive near the Colline Gate at a place afterwards called the Accursed Plain—presumably from this event. [5] At the time of the Second Punic War, two Vestals, Opimia and Floronia, violated their vows of chastity, and were detected: one committed suicide, the other was buried alive at the Colline Gate. Lucius Cantilius, one of the clerks of the pontiffs, charged with a liaison with Floronia, was scourged to death. [6] Catiline was accused of incest with a Vestal, a half-sister of Cicero's wife; but she was acquitted, probably because of influential friends. [7] We are not surprised to read that Nero, who had no regard for anything sacred, deflowered a Vestal. [8] Juvenal, with a contemptuous sneer, accused Crispinus of a liaison with a Vestal; [9] but Domitian's interest in Crispinus prevented the traditional punishment for the crime. Incest with Vestals seems to have been condoned by Vespasian and Titus; [10] but Suetonius tells us that Domitian visited offenders, at first with capital punishment, and later on with the extreme penalty, burial alive. Oculata and Varronilla broke their vows, and Domitian allowed them to choose their mode of death. Their lovers suffered banishment. Cornelia, the chief of the Vestals, had been acquitted once; but she was accused again, convicted, and buried alive, and her paramours were beaten to death with rods. One, an ex-praetor, was allowed to go into exile. In at least one instance—that of the Vestal Posturnia—the charge of unchastity was quashed; but, as Livy says, [11] she was under suspicion because of her free and easy manner. We recall that Vestals were supposed to dress modestly in white, to keep their eyes on the ground and their thoughts on holy things.

Colorable offenses of the Vestals were punished as follows: [12] the Vestal was stripped and placed in a dark place. The Chief Priest, with an arras between him and the peccant Vestal, lashed her with thongs to drive out the evil as well as to punish her. When a Vestal broke her vow of chastity a terrible fate awaited her if she could not prove her innocence or if she had no influential friends to espouse her cause. She was buried alive in a small underground chamber located within the city walls, at one of the gates. She was stripped of her sacred fillets, tied down on a covered litter in such a way that she might utter no sound, and conveyed to the Great Roman Forum, where the people who attended the litter made way for her to pass. When the procession arrived at the tomb, the Chief Priest loosened the cords which bound her, and, raising his hands toward the sky, prayed inaudibly. Then he brought the Vestal from the litter and laid her on the steps of the tomb. She then descended by a ladder into the subterranean room and was left to die, with the small comfort, however, of a bed, a lamp, some bread, milk and water; for since she had been consecrated to religion, it would have been impious to allow her to die of hunger.

Among many peoples, there is supposed to exist some connection between fertility in women and fertility in the earth. This is not difficult to understand when we remember that among savage peoples the men are engaged in hunting, fishing, and fighting, while the women plough and sow. This connection is suggested, for example, by the common practice [13] of throwing products of the earth, such as rice, at marriage ceremonies and at the birth of children. A Roman bride who desired to be prolific should be wed, as the superstition went, "in the very bosom of Mother Earth, among the ripened crops, above the fruitful soil." [14] The fertility of the earth and of the crops would thus be communicated to the bride.

At several Roman festivals whose purpose was to assist the ripening of the crops, abstinence from sexual intercourse was enjoined upon the worshipers. Thus during the nine nights of the Fes-

tival of Ceres married women must not touch a man. [15] At the
Festival of the Ambarvalia no one who had had sexual intercourse the night before might approach the altar. [16] Inasmuch as
primitive people thus closely associate the fertility of women with
the fertility of the soil, the lashing of women at the Lupercalia may
well have been intended to promote fertility in the crops. Again, in
the rites of the Argei, which were closely connected with crops, and
at the Festival of Pales, the Vestals had important functions. [17] At the
Festival of Vesta, they offered sacred cakes, made in the primitive
way by the three eldest Vestals out of the first grain garnered in
May. [18] The burying of Vestals when they had broken their vows of
chastity, then, may conceivably have been a sacrifice to the Earth
whose products they were likely to harm by their immorality. Ovid
himself comes close to this interpretation when he says: [19] "Thus
the unchaste Vestal perishes, because she is buried in that earth
which she contaminated. For Earth and Vesta are the same divinity."

We have the definite statement of Propertius [20] that there was
a connection between sexual purity and good crops. At Lanuvium, in
a grove of Juno the Savior, there was a pit in which a hungry snake
awaited his yearly feast of barley cakes. These cakes were carried in
baskets by maidens who were blindfolded and then lowered into the
pit. If the girls were pure, the snake snatched away the food. Thus
proved to be virgins, they returned home to their parents, while the
shepherds cried out in joy, "The year will be fruitful." If, however, the
girls were impure and the snake refused their gifts of food, they were
punished by law—perhaps, as in the case of the Vestals, by being
buried alive. Thus the rite was not only a test of the virginity of the

maidens, but their purity had some mysterious effect in assuring good crops. The same reason, as we have seen, may be given for the sacrifice of the Vestals who broke their vow of chastity.

There is a modern parallel among the Ibibio in southern Nigeria, who wipe out the pollution of adultery by sacrifice to the Earth or to their ancestors. [21]

In some Roman rites, abstinence from sexual intercourse was required, especially on the eve of a religious festival. The wife of the Priest of Jupiter must not have touched her husband until after the ceremony of cleansing in the temple of Vesta. [22] We have seen that during the Festival of Ceres women had to sleep alone. [23] The same prohibition applied to the worshipers in the Festival of Bacchus, also a god of one of the products of the earth. [24] Here again, in rites of an agricultural nature, sexual purity was necessary for the good of the crops. The Emperor Severus Alexander would regularly worship his Lares early in the morning, unless he had lain with his wife the night before. [25]

Cooks, bakers, butlers must be chaste. [26] If one was sexually impure he had to wash in a running stream before touching the contents of the storeroom. We have already observed that beekeepers, before handling their hives, had to refrain from sexual intercourse. Frazer gives us an interestmg parallel. He writes: [27] "The Masai think that if the couple were to break the rule of continence while the wine is brewing, not only would the wine be undrinkable but the bees which made the honey would fly away." In such cases as these of course, the person does not know why he observes the taboo. At any rate the taboo on sexual intercourse among savages, as well as among civilized peoples, is required of persons engaged in occupations necessary for the good of the community. [28]

In Oriental rites abstinence was a familiar requirement for worshipers. In the case of Isis, a ten days' abstinence was demanded, as we learn from the restive complaint of Propertius: [29] "The rites of Isis are now returning again to give me gloom; for Cynthia ten nights now has been continually engaged in worship." Tibullus similarly lamented the fact that Delia was separated from him during her observance of the rites of Isis. [30] Among the Gauls, too, persons who were chaste were most acceptable in religious rites. [31] The sexual purity of children may account for their employment in these rites. Thus children were used to bring provisions from the sacred storeroom. [32]

The taboo on sex is difficult to explain. Generally speaking, however, we may ascribe it to the belief that the weakness following upon the sexual act will be communicated to the religious rite or to the action proposed. Specifically, in the case of the Vestals, the prohibition is referable to the principles of sympathetic magic. Assume a belief in the connection between chastity and the fertility of the crops, and that is sufficient to cause the prohibition. In some cases there may be originally a biological reason corresponding to the period after detumescence, when the savage would naturally be chaste. Thus chastity before certain religious rites would be an unconscious—instinctive, if you will—conservation of the sexual strength for expression during the festival involving the fertility of the crops.

Men

Men were, naturally, debarred from rites in which women's interests were especially involved. The taboo on men in such cases is due to the fact that they were strange creatures, physiologically unlike women, and so potentially dangerous. Hence the presence of men in women's rites interferes with their efficacy. This was particularly the case in the Festival of the Good Goddess (Bona Dea). The temple of this divinity had been dedicated by an heiress of the Claudian family who had never had intercourse with a man. [33] We recall that the notorious Clodius, dressed as a music girl, entered the house of Julius Caesar with the connivance of Caesar's wife when the rites were being held there. This sacrilege was a first-rate scandal at the time and led to Caesar's divorcing his wife Pompeia. [34] Again, all men, except the Chief Priest, were prohibited from the worship of Vesta. [35] A curious instance of this taboo is recorded in one of Pliny's letters. [36] When the Vestal Cornelia, who had been accused of breaking her vows, was descending into her living tomb, her dress caught. The public executioner turned as if to disentangle it, but Cornelia drew back shuddering "as if to ward off the foul contagion from her chaste and pure body." Men were allowed to worship at all the shrines of Diana except one in the Patrician Quarter of Rome. The reason, as given by Plutarch, [37] is that a man had once tried to deflower a woman in the temple and had been torn to pieces by the dogs. Thereafter men avoided the temple.

Strangers

Cicero explicitly states that the Romans had an aversion to foreigners. [38] Servius says that in ancient days the Romans seldom welcomed strangers unless they had the "right of hospitality" (ius hospitii). [39] The uncanny feeling which the Romans had from early times in the presence of their Italian neighbors is shown by the fact that they associated sorcery with the Marsians—the leaders of the Italian allies in the war for the Roman franchise. They were believed to have descended from Circe and to have inherited her magic powers. [40] Again, the sons of King Ancus considered it an outrage that the Roman State should fall into the hands of a foreigner. [41]

The Roman's feeling toward his enemies is well illustrated by the words of a consul during the Second Punic War, who accused Hannibal's soldiers of eating human flesh. Even to touch these men, he felt, would be an act of impiety. [42] After the defection of the city of Capua to Hannibal and its subsequent capture by the Romans in 211 B.c., the statues which the Romans had purloined from the city were placed in the hands of the College of Priests, presumably to be purified from contact with the enemy. [43] Some notion of taboo may lie behind the expulsion of the foreign Volscians from the sacred games in Rome in 491 B.c. The Volscians, at least, so interpreted it. [44] The brother of Scipio the Elder was once fined for some reason or other, and he was given the choice of furnishing security or going to jail. A tribune—the father of the famous Tiberius and Gaius Gracchus—saved him from prison by his veto on the ground that the prison had been contaminated by enemy prisoners. This feeling of danger from contamination by foreigners was a sufficiently strong motive to use as a pretext to save Scipio's brother. [45]

In one religious rite, of whose nature, however, we know nothing, it is expressly stated that the stranger must depart from the sacrifice. [46] The Romans had many requirements which the young girl who aspired to be a Vestal had to meet: among them, that her father must have his residence in Italy. [47] In certain rites at Iguvium, a procession about the town was made by the Fratres Attiedii. From these rites foreigners were excluded. "Send beyond the boundaries the Tadinate people, the Tadinate tribe, the Tuscan and the Narcan folk, the Iapudic folk (saying), 'if any remain, then bring (such person) whither it is lawful to bring him, do unto him as it is lawful to do.'" [48]

We have already seen that certain priests called verbenarii went with the Roman armies into foreign lands, bearing with them the sacred herbs which were used to disinfect the army from contagion of blood and foreign influences. [49] One of the war-heralds in the ceremony of treaty-making took the sacred herbs from the citadel and touched the head of the chief herald to keep him free from contamination. [50]

A curious case of taboo, germane to the taboo on strangers, is found in Livy's account of early Rome. In 445 B.C., a tribune proposed a bill to legalize marriage between the plebeians and the patricians. The consuls opposed the measure on the ground that, if it were allowed, religion would be thrown into confusion and nothing would be left uncontaminated. From the patrician point of view, the plebeians were taboo and hence dangerous to the religious system. At any rate, so they interpreted the point for the edification of the plebeians, whom they wanted to keep from usurping their immemorial rites. Again, the election of a plebeian consul was looked upon as impious. [51] In the consulship of Marcus Valerius and Quintus Apuleius an attempt was made on the part of the plebeians to secure representation in the college of augurs and pontiffs. The patricians were against the measure, contending that the gods would oppose such contamination. [52]

It seems odd that among the Romans, as well as among other ancient peoples and among savages of our own day, strangers, who are ordinarily taboo, should often be treated with great consideration; [53] but the explanation is quite simple. As the stranger possesses mana which is at least potentially dangerous, he must be prevented from doing barm; and this end is attained by feeding and housing him. [54] The Malays, we read, [55] fear the Jakuns who are skilled in magic and can, by striking two sticks together, cause an enemy to die. But they can do good, too; and for this reason the Malays treat the Jakuns with respect.

Casar writes the following concerning the Germans: [56] "They do not think it right to violate a guest; those who, for whatever cause, have come to them, they keep from harm and hold sacred; the houses of all are open to them; with them food is shared." The Germans housed and fed the stranger as if he were their own; and thus becoming one of them in reality, he was no longer able to do them harm. The Romans thus welcomed foreign gods within their gates, albeit outside the sacred pomerium. [57]

Slaves

The presence of slaves was believed to interfere with the efficacy of many religious rites, both Greek and Roman. [58] The Romans, for example, had to repeat the Great Games of 491 B.c., because, on the morning set for the games, a citizen had driven a recalcitrant slave through the circus where the games were to be held. [59] It appears that the young rake Clodius flooded with slaves the theater where games in honor of the Great Mother were being held—a pollution which angered his arch-enemy Cicero. [60] The rites of Hercules at the Greatest Altar in the Cattle Market were, for many years, performed by members of two distinguished Roman families. One family, however, seems to have gained the chief control of the cult and to have delegated the performance of the rites to certain public slaves. As a punishment for this pollution by contact with slaves, the family died out. [61] Among the qualifications necessary for a Vestal was that neither of her parents might have been a slave. [62]

Slave women were excluded from the temple of the Goddess of the Morning (Mater Matuta), whom the Romans identified with the Greek goddess Ino-Leucothea, because of many similarities in ritual, and myth. Each free woman, however, might bring a slave girl into the sacred precincts, but she had to slap the face of the girl before doing so. [63] The slap on the face may be considered a magic transfer, for the occasion only, of the freedom of the mistress to the slave. Similar temporary manumissions occurred at the Festival of Saturn and at the Festival of the Lares of the Crossroads (Compitalia). At this latter festival, the overseer was the sacrificer, apparently for the slaves of the family. [64] Slaves were also admitted to the rites of Fors Fortuna. The reason, as stated by Ovid, was that Servius Tullius, the founder of the temple, had been born a slave. [65] Despite the taboo on slaves in religious worship, it seems that a slave might have the right of refuge at the statue of a god. [66] Slaves were allowed to take part in rites in honor of the dead. [67]

The Emperor Claudius offered a public prayer whenever a bird of ill omen appeared on the Capitol. From this rite he ordered all slaves and artisans to withdraw. [68] Nero, in 60 A.D., instituted games on the model of the Olympic Games; and while considerable license was allowed, pantomime actors, being slaves, were excluded because of the religious character of the games. [69]

The taboo on slaves seems to have been partly an artificial one. It may have been fostered by the free people in order to keep religious matters strictly in their own hands. The fact that slaves were usually foreigners may have been a contributing cause.

Linen and Wool

That the Romans had an uncanny feeling with regard to linen is suggested occasionally in their literature. Corpses, for instance, were regularly shrouded in linen. [70] This in itself would be sufficient to invest linen with harmful mana. After the bones of a cremated body had been sprinkled with wine and soaked in milk, the moisture was removed with linen cloths. [71] It is possible that the linen on the breastplate of a Roman soldier had magical significance, probably warding off the spirits of the enemies slain in battle. [72] Just before Galba was assassinated, he put on a linen cuirass, "although openly averring that it would avail little against so many swords." [73] He probably felt that the only help it could give him was magical. The Roman standards may have been of linen. [74]

In religious rites linen was usually taboo. Servius states [75] that linen was "foreign to Roman ritual." The heralds who were entrusted with the responsibility of declaring war and making treaties were not allowed to wear linen garments. [76] Again, if the wife of the Priest of Jupiter sewed her woolen garment with a linen thread, she had to perform an atoning sacrifice.

In spite of Servius' words, linen was occasionally used in religious rites. We have a definite statement of the Emperor Marcus Aurelius to this effect, in a letter written to his old teacher Fronto, where, among other things, he writes about a certain town: [77] "There was no corner without a shrine, a holy place, a temple. Besides, many books of linen were to be found in the temples, and the linen was of religious significance." He describes these books as sacra, not as religiosa. The latter adjective, as we have already noted, was regularly used in the sense of taboo, particularly the taboo on death. Sacer, too, often has the same connotation; but in this passage the context seems to demand sacra in the usual sense of "holy." A possible explanation may be that the taboo on linen began gradually to disappear under the Empire because of the growing familiarity with its use in Oriental cults. However, Marcus Aurelius' remark on the religious importance of the linen in the books naturally suggests that he had some reason for mentioning the fact to Fronto: possibly Fronto had usually associated some feeling of taboo with linen. The rolls containing the names of the magistrates, which were kept in the temple of Juno Moneta, were called "linen books." [78] Again, a Roman consul who had won a victory over the Samnites forced the vanquished enemy to serve in his army, using novel religious rites at their induction. These soldiers made up his "linen legion," so called because the sacrifice of induction was made in an enclosure covered with linen; and the forms used in the ritual were read by an old priest from a linen book. [79] The explanation of these rites is similar to that of the presence of linen on the breastplate of the Roman soldier. The soldiers were foreigners, and hence were taboo to a Roman. The rites were magical, intended to drive away evil forces which were felt to be attached to foreigners.

Sometimes an uncanny association was attached to wool. Thus there is record of a rain of wool following upon the death of a distinguished Roman. [80] Fillets worn by the priests and priestesses were commonly made of wool. [81] In the case of the Vestals they were tokens of chastity. Ovid mentions [82] wool among the instruments of purification called februa. The wife of the Priest of Jupiter wore a kind of veil on her head at sacrifices; to this was attached a spray of the pomegranate tree, the two ends of which were fastened with wool. [83] The envoy who went to the borders to demand satisfaction of a nation which had wronged the Roman people wore a woolen covering on his head. [84]

Wool was regularly used in Roman religious rites. At the Festival of the Lares of the Crossroads, woolen images of men and women and balls of wool—the images representing all free men and women, the balls representing all slaves—were suspended at night at the crossroads and probably also at the housedoors. These represented a substitute for an earlier human sacrifice to the spirits of the dead in the underworld who might harm the living. Festus says: [85] " ... As many balls as there are slaves and as many effigies as there are freeborn men and women in the family are set up, that the spirits may spare the living and be content with these balls as substitutes." That human sacrifice prevailed in Rome up to 97 B.C. is proved by a decree of the Senate of that year which provided "that no human being be immolated..." [86] In the rites of the Sacrifice of the Pregnant Cow (Fordicidia), Ovid represents Numa slaying two ewes, whose fleece he spreads on the ground, and on these he lies in worshiping Faunus. [87]

The fact that linen was commonly used by priests in Oriental cults, not only for clothing but as a veil for sacred things, may have tended to add negative mana to it at Rome where wool was normally worn in religious rites. In the tale of Thelyphron, for instance, which we related in our first chapter, [88] the Egyptian prophet who brought the corpse to life was clad in linen. We know that the worshipers of Isis dressed in linen. [89] Apuleius, who was initiated into the mysteries of Isis and Osiris, calls linen "the purest covering for divine things." [90] Wool, he reminds us, was considered unclean by the followers of Orpheus and Pythagoras. The Jewish prophets wore linen. [91] In Leviticus we read the specifications for the high priest's dress: [92] "He shall put on the holy linen coat, and he shall have the linen breeches upon his flesh, and shall be girded with a linen girdle, and with the linen mitre shall he be attired: these are holy garments ..."

We have seen, then, that the Romans had an uncanny feeling

about the presence of linen in religious rites because of its association with dead bodies and with magic, particularly the magic of aversion in the case of the spirits of slain enemies. We have seen, too, that linen was regularly worn by devotees of Oriental cults and that this would have a tendency to increase the danger of a material which was already endowed, for other reasons, with negative mana. Thus the taboo on linen may be closely linked up with the taboos on death and on the stranger. Furthermore, wool was commonly used in religious rites, and since wool was the older material, the gods would naturally be averse to adopting linen, which was new and was associated with death, magic, and foreign rites.

Knots

Rites of binding and tying and the use of knots were common in Roman magic. For example, while his sweetheart Delia lay ill, Tibullus performed magic rites for her recovery and made nine vows to Trivia, "his head veiled in wool and with loosened tunic." [93] Images of lovers, which were employed by witches, were commonly bound with magic threads. [94] Belief in the dangerous character of knots of all sorts, in religious rites, is not confined to any one people. Frazer writes, for instance: [95] "... among the gypsies of Transylvania, as soon as the birth-pains set in, every knot is untied, not only on the clothes of the woman in labor, but also on everything in her neighborhood. . . ."

We know that knots, as well as things tied or bound, were considered harmful in all religious rites among the Romans. This may have been due to fear that the binding principle would be carried over to the rites and hinder their effectiveness. Servius, in his commentary on Vergil's Aeneid, [96] says: " ... In sacred rites, it is customary for nothing to be bound." The requirement that women must have their hair flowing and their garments ungirt in all religious rites is attributable to the taboo on knots. The wife of the Priest of Jupiter must leave her hair untouched by a comb on at least three occasions: during the ceremonial procession among the shrines called Argei, [97] at the Festival of Vesta until the Tiber had carried the sweepings from the temple of Vesta to the sea, [98] and during the ritualistic "moving" of the shields in March. [99] At funerals women wore their hair streaming and their garments had to be ungirt. [100] A pregnant woman loosened her hair before praying to Juno Lucina, a goddess of childbirth, in order "that the goddess might tenderly release her child." [101] Knots in any form were forbidden at the rites of this deity. [102] Crossing of the legs or fingers was considered harmful to pregnant women. [103] A person who was minded to do one harm could be forestalled by crossing the legs and intertwining the fingers. [104] Dido, in preparing for self-destruction, pretended to her sister Anna that she was performing magic rites to destroy her lover. We read: [105] "Dido calls to witness the gods—having freed one foot of its sandal, and with garment ungirt." The reason for thus baring her foot and loosing her dress is, as Servius thinks, [106] "that she may be freed and AEneas be entangled."

The Priest of Jupiter must have no knots on his conical cap, his girdle, or any part of his dress. [107] He was forbidden to touch ivy or to walk under vines, probably because of the grasping knotty character of their tendrils. [108] In Livy's account of the inauguration of Numa, representing, no doubt, that of a typical Roman priest, we read [109] that the curved wand of the augur must be without a knot. The worshipers at the festival of the Lemuria must have nothing binding on their feet. [110] The sacrificial animal had to be led to the altar by a rope in which there was no knot. [111] Animals were unyoked at country festivals, and the sacrificial victim must be one that had never touched a yoke or been mated. [112]

A curious case of taboo is recorded by Pliny the Elder. [113] According to the law of most country districts in Italy, women were not permitted to spin or to carry their spindles uncovered as they walked on the highroads, for the crops would be harmed thereby. The reason for this taboo seems to be that as the threads became tangled on the spindle, so, by the principle of sympathy, the crops would become tangled with weeds. Again, for the same reason, women were not allowed to spin at the time of the Festival of the Ambarvalia. [114]

Similarly rings, which, like knots, were commonly used in magic rites, were taboo. The Priest of Jupiter was not allowed to wear a ring unless it was broken and stoneless. [115] In the religious rites which Numa performs in the sacred grove of Faunus, as described by Ovid, the king is forbidden to wear a ring. [116]

In all the instances cited—whether the taboo be on rings, dressed hair, crossed legs, crossed fingers, fettered culprit, peasant's spindle, or actual knots in clothes or rope—the same principle is involved: as the ring, the crossed legs, the fetters, the spindle, the knot, bind physically, so they bind the god and his rites—a survival of the earliest days when man believed that a thing or action which resembled another thing or action (whether actual or conceived in the imagination) was one and the same thing.

Servius has an inkling of the principle in his comments on the lines of Vergil which describe the priest Helenus removing his sacred fillets before approaching the temple of Apollo: [117] "In the procedure of sacred rites, this (i.e. the removing of the fillets) is appropriate both for soul and body; for generally those things which cannot be done with respect to the soul can be done with respect to the body—as loosing or binding—that the soul may, from resemblance, perceive what it cannot of itself perceive." The priest Helenus laid aside his fillets, and, thus removing the binding principle, he was free to receive the inspiration of the god.

We know that knots and rings were commonly used in magic, especially in rites intended to bind lovers together; and so it may be barely possible that the priests of the Roman State religion deliberately discouraged objects and actions which belonged to popular rites of magic. Whether this be true or not, the Romans had a feeling that knots had some evil influence on religious rites; hence they avoided them. The most natural explanation of the taboo is on the principle of similarity.

Iron and Bronze

The taboo on iron dates from the beginning of the Iron Age when religious conservatism forbade the use of the strange new material in place of the usual bronze. [118] It has been suggested that the magic significance of iron arose from its susceptibility to magnetism which, as the superstitious Romans often believed, it derived from witchcraft. [119] The Romans believed that the lodestone recruited its strength from iron. Roman priests, in at least one instance, used the lodestone's powers to bring about a mysterious attraction between an iron image of Mars—presumably a small one—and an image of Venus, made of lodestone. [120] Thus did the priests blithely employ science for their own ends.

In many magic rites, iron early lost its power to harm. In the charm, for instance, which Cato has left us in his treatise on agriculture, iron figured in a helpful way. We give Cato's directions for inducing a broken or a dislocated bone to come together: [121]

"If a bone has been dislocated, it will become whole by this charm. Take a green reed, four or five feet long; split it in the middle, and let two men hold the pieces against the hip joints. Begin to chant: 'Motas vaeta daries dardares astataries dissunapiter,' until the pieces of the reed come together. Keep tossing iron above. When the pieces of the reed have come together, and the one touches the other, seize them with the hand, and cut them right and left; bind them to the dislocation or to the fracture, and it will become sound. And yet every day chant (as above), or in the following manner: 'Huat haut huat istasis tarsis ardannabou dannaustra.'"

This is a piece of sheer magic. As the two split pieces of reed come together, so the broken pieces of the bone will mend. The element in the rite that concerns us especially here, however, is the tossing of iron above the broken bone. The iron apparently is used to ward off any evil influences which might hinder the mending of the bone. We find a similar use of iron in the case of the Priest of Jupiter, who placed a piece of iron under his pillow at night in order to ward off evil influences. [122] A like superstition had it that iron, placed beneath the straw on which hens had dropped their eggs, would keep the eggs from spoiling. [123]

Another quality of iron may, along with its magnetic powers, help to account for its taboo in certain rites. Man must have noticed at a very early time that sparks flew from iron and stone when they were struck together.

The Arval Brothers were originally forbidden to use iron implements for engraving inscriptions in their sacred grove. They therefore performed an atoning sacrifice with a lamb and a pig in advance, in order to avoid the displeasure which the gods might feel because of their having used an iron graving tool. The atoning sacrifice was made again when the iron instrument was taken from the grove. [124] Similarly, no iron implement could be used in repairing the Sublician Bridge, which was made entirely of wood and fastened with wooden pins. [125] While it seems probable that the prohibition here is a religious one, there is a possibility, as Pliny suggests, [126] that it may have been necessary in order to facilitate tearing the bridge down quickly at the approach of an enemy. There was a similar taboo on iron at the building of the temple of Solomon. [127] In the regulations of the temple of Jupiter Liber at Furfo a special provision was made allowing iron to be used in repairing the temple, showing that there must have been some misgivings as to the propriety of its use. [128]

Servius records [129] that if a man bound in chains entered the house of a flamen he must be loosened from his chains and that these had to be lowered through the skylight into the street. Here, not only the fact that the man was bound and in chains of iron made him dangerous, but also the fact that he was a criminal; for criminals were regularly taboo in Rome. [130]

In historical times, bronze was commonly used in magic as well as in religious rites. Vergil, for instance, represents [131] Dido pretending to consult a witch who cuts herbs by moonlight with a bronze sickle. In the magic rites of the Silent Goddess, Tacita (to which we shall return in a later chapter), an old witch sews up the head of a small fish with a bronze needle, in order by sympathetic magic to bind the lips of a slanderous person. [132] Marcellus Empiricus, in his directions for the preparation of amulets, includes implements of reed, of copper, and of glass, but not of iron. [133] We know that both Etruscans and Romans used only bronze ploughshares to dig furrows in founding their cities; [134] and their priests, as well as those of the Sabines, used bronze razors. [135] The hair and nails of the Priest of Jupiter must be cut, not with iron, but with a bronze knife. [136] The dress worn by the flamens while offering sacrifice was fastened with a clasp of bronze. [137] The Leaping Priests of Mars wore bronze corselets. [138] While Italy was being threatened by the Goths, there was an eclipse, and the night rang with wailings and the beating of bronze. [139] Again, during the revolt of the Roman soldiers in Pannonia, an eclipse of the moon caused panic in the camp. The air rang with the crash of trumpets and other bronze implements. These were calculated, as Tacitus says, [140] to aid the moon in her labors; but, as a modern scholar has recently suggested, [141] they may have been believed to drive away the goblin which was swallowing up the moon.

Places

That certain places were affected by the feeling of taboo we have already shown; and the reason for the uncanny feeling in each case was that associated with the place was a particular form of taboo: in the case of burial grounds, for instance, the taboo on the corpse.

Thunder and lightning have always caused feelings of uneasiness among men, whether savage or civilized. Juvenal, for instance, writes: [142] "There are those who tremble and blanch at every lightning flash; and when it thunders they are helpless even on the first rumbling in the sky." It is not strange, then, that places struck by lightning should be considered taboo by the Romans. Such places were surrounded with a low well-shaped wall and marked with an inscription indicating that the thunderbolt had been duly buried. [143] A lamb was sacrificed in expiation. [144] There seems to have been a college of priests whose duty was properly to care for the rites of "burying the thunderbolt." [145] On one occasion the temples of Jupiter and Minerva were struck by lightning and Nero, on the advice of soothsayers, purified the whole city. [146] The Emperor Galba's grandfather once performed an expiatory sacrifice after a place had been struck by lightning. [147] According to the laws of Numa, a man who had been struck by lightning must not be lifted above the knees and no rites of burial could be performed. [148] Such a man might not be cremated and must be buried, presumably on the spot where he had been struck. [149]

Many taboos on places arose from particular events which had proved disastrous. For instance, there was a taboo on the right-hand passage of the Carmental Gate because the three hundred and six members of the Fabian family had passed through it to fight against the Veii, never to return. [150] Gervasius von Tilbury furnishes us with a parallel from Naples. [151] He and a friend tried to enter the city by the lefthand side of the city gate, when an ass, laden with wood, blocked the way and forced the travelers to use the right side. On reaching the home of their host, the latter inquired by which side of the gate they had entered, and, when he learned that they had used the right-hand side, he said: "Every one who enters the city by the right-hand side will succeed in whatever business he has in hand; every one on the contrary who enters on the left will find and meet with nothing but disappointment." The dusty traveler for the moment began to yield to the superstition; but catching himself he muttered piously: "In Thy hands, O Lord, are all things, and there is nothing that can resist Thy power."

We have in the last two chapters treated the following taboos in Roman life: blood, women, children, death and corpses, sex, men, strangers, slaves, linen, knots, iron, and places. Of these, the taboo on blood has been found to have arisen either from instinct or because of the association of death and suffering with its presence; that on women and children from the fact that they are weak physically, and this weakness, by the familiar law of association by similarity, may be communicated to the religious rite, affecting it adversely. Furthermore, the presence of blood at menstruation and at the birth of the child adds to women and children the uncanniness of blood. That on corpses may be attributed to man's instinct for self-preservation; the strangeness of the dead body may add to its mysterious character; moreover, man associates death with the agonies of the last moments of the sick man, and hence fears death. The taboo on sexual intercourse may perhaps best be explained on the ground that after the sexual act comes a period of weakness which will be communicated magically to the religious rite or to the actions of daily life. The taboo on men is due to their physical unlikeness to women; that on strangers may be due both to the fact that what is new or unfamiliar is dangerous and to the association of ideas of death and blood and pain with the stranger. That on slaves seems to have been entirely artificial; but, inasmuch as slaves were foreigners, the taboo on strangers may apply here also. The taboo on linen may be due to its association with corpses, to its strangeness in comparison with wool (the older material), and to its use in Oriental rites—a taboo, therefore, on that which is foreign. The taboo on knots is obvious: the principle of sympathetic magic holds here. As the knot binds, so the action is bound. The taboo on iron is due to its strangeness at the time when it was introduced, to its susceptibility to magnetism, and to its power of producing sparks when struck. The taboo on places has no one origin. The uncanniness of each place has a special cause: contact with death, association with disaster, and the like.

CHAPTER IV
Magic Acts: The General Principles

Homoeopathic and Contagious Magic

WE HAVE observed, in our first chapter, that magic acts arise from early man's inability to distinguish effect from cause, the part from the whole, that which is like or has been in contact with a person or thing, from the person or thing itself, imaginings about facts from the facts themselves. These turns in thinking, which seem so odd to us, we have ascribed to man's ignorance of the world in which he finds himself—all of which makes him unable to distinguish error from truth. That early man's brain was underdeveloped physiologically may, in a measure, account for this inability to form correct associations and to make logical inferences. However, the precarious life of the savage and the dangers with which he is beleaguered tend to heighten his inability to think correctly.

Note an example, taken from modern times, of such incorrect thinking. Andrew Lang is our informant. He writes: [1] " ... the arrival of the French missionaries among the Hurons was coincident with certain unfortunate events; therefore it was argued that the advent of the missionaries was the cause of the misfortune." And one example taken from antiquity. Aulus Gellius [2] once attended a dinner given by a poet friend at which shriveled oysters were served. The host thus explained: "The moon, you see, is now waning; oysters, therefore, like certain other things, are scrawny and juiceless." The eyes of cats, too, Gellius informs us, grow larger or smaller according to whether the moon is waxing or waning.

When a person imitates the evil he would repel—grinning like a wolf to ward off wolves, smearing his face with blood to ward off blood and death, making thunderous noises to drive away thunder-storms—anthropologists speak of homoeopathic magic; when he makes use of some object, such as hair or nails, which has been a part of or has been in contact with the individual, the name contagious magic is given. The general term sympathetic magic is applied to both types, for a mysterious sympathy is supposed to exist between the object to be influenced and the object which is like or has been in contact with it. Often the rite is both contagious and homoeopathic at the same time.

In our introductory chapter we discussed one example, taken from primitive magic, of the principles stated above. We shall now add to this an account of two magic rites which, while having no organic connection with the Roman State religion, yet occurred in connection with State rites.

On June first—a day known as the Kalends of the Beans—the pontiffs sacrificed to a somewhat obscure goddess of great antiquity, Carna, the "Flesh Goddess," in an ancient grove near the Tiber. [3] The goddess, it would seem, had in her care the vital organs of human beings, the heart, liver, and stomach. There was a shrine to Carna on the Caelian Hill which, as the tradition went, Marcus Junius Brutus, in fulfillment of a vow, dedicated to her after the expulsion of Tarquin the Proud. Beans mixed with spelt were sacrificed to Carna because, as Macrobius says, "by these foods especially the powers of the human body are strengthened." The people ate this mixture and fat bacon, foods which, they believed, prevented stomach disorders. [4]

We may dismiss, as W. Warde Fowler has done, [5] Ovid's identification of Carna with Cardea, the goddess of the hinge; for quite obviously Ovid made the identification in order to introduce a racy story into his text.

We are particularly interested here in Carna as she survived in popular belief, long after the goddess had ceased to be worshiped. She possessed the powers of a witch and could be invoked to keep off bloodsucking vampires which appeared in the form of screech owls. The rites of riddance, described by Ovid in the case of the infant Procas who became king of Alba Longa, are as follows: [6]

"Immediately she (Crane) touches the doorposts three times in succession with a spray of arbutus; three times she marks the threshold with an arbutus spray. She sprinkles the entrance with water (and the water contained a drug). She holds the bloody entrails of a two months' old sow and thus speaks: 'Birds of the night, spare the entrails of the boy. For a small boy a small victim falls. Take heart for heart, I pray, entrails for entrails. This life we give you in place of a better one.'"

Having killed the sow, the witch placed the vital organs in the open air and forbade those attending the rite to look upon them. Then a whitethorn branch was set in a small window which furnished light to the house. After that the child was safe and the color returned to his pallid face.

The principle of similarity in this magic act is evident: the vital organs of the child, which, in early Roman times, were under the care of the goddess Carna, are to be saved by the vicarious offering of a sow. The pig was frequently thus used. A similar substitution is to be seen in the ceremony of treaty-making, preserved in Livy, where the spokesman for the Roman side strikes a sacrificial pig, uttering these words the while: [7] "If (the Roman people) shall be the first to defect (from the terms of the treaty) ... then do you, Diespiter, so strike the Roman people as I shall here to-day strike this pig."

In the magic rites of Crane there is no mention of a divinity—an important fact, of which we shall take notice in our next chapter. The significant elements of the description for our present use are the sprinkling of purificatory waters, the striking of the doorpost and the threshold with arbutus, and the placing of the spray of whitethorn in the window. The belief that whitethorn could keep off the spirits was common in antiquity. Ovid, in the rite which we have just described, says [8] that "by it she (the witch) could drive away sorrow-bringing harm from the doors." The Greeks had such a belief. [9] So, too, many country people in our day use whitethorn to avert evils. [10] Striking and sweeping are universal methods of dispelling evil influences. Hence the witch swept the threshold and the window sill where the vampires would naturally seek entrance.

Another example: On the twenty-first of February, the Feralia, a day on which Roman families concluded their rites in honor of the dead, occurred a curious bit of magic which was intended to silence an enemy. It had no official connection with the ritual of the day, but was appropriate perhaps because, as Frazer facetiously remarks, [11] "the dead ... are notoriously silent." The picture which Ovid draws [12] is that of an old beldame, surrounded by a group of girls, performing magic rites to Tacita, the Silent Goddess. With three fingers she places three pinches of incense in a mouse's hole under the threshold, probably an offering to the spirits of the dead, which are commonly believed to haunt thresholds. [13] Then, as she utters a spell, she winds woolen threads about a dark-colored lead image of the person whose slanderous tongue she is endeavoring to seal up. Meanwhile, she turns black beans in her mouth. She then takes a fish and smears its head with pitch, pierces it with a bronze needle, and sews it up. As she leaves, she utters these words: "Hostile tongues and enemy lips have we bound."

We have several of the usual magic details in this rite: the number three, incense, beans, woolen threads, the color black, the lead image, bronze, spinning. The object of the performance is to keep a slanderous person from talking. This is accomplished, first, by winding woolen threads around a leaden image of the slanderer. As the old woman thus binds the image, she binds the slanderer. Am incantation assists the magic act. As the mouth of the fish is sewed up, so the mouth of the slanderer will be sealed. The use of the fish in this case is clear: as the person to be affected by the magic is to be rendered silent, a silent creature must be chosen to represent him. Again, thresholds are favorite haunts of departed spirits: hence the appropriateness of the incense offering at that spot.

It is interesting to know in this connection that the punishment meted out in hell by Minos to persons who had been talkative and betrayed secrets was that they should become fishes, that thus, in unending silence, they might atone for the wagging of their tongues. [14]

Whether there was actually a goddess Tacita is problematic.

Plutarch [15] calls her one of the Muses and says that Numa instituted her worship in honor of the silence enjoined by Pythagoras upon his followers.

We turn now to magic rain-making. We shall first take two examples from Christianity, one from ancient and one from modern times, and one example from modern China. Then we shall discuss a Roman rite of rain-making.

When Marcus Aurelius was leading his forces against the Quadi in 174 A.D., a drought settled upon their country. According to one account, some Christians who happened to be serving under the Roman standards prayed for rain, and forthwith the heavens overflowed. [16] The pagan account of this rainstorm says that an Egyptian magician procured it from Hermes. [17] We do not have to go to antiquity, however, for evidence of supernatural rain-making. Frazer records [18] a case of rain-making by immersing the statue of a saint in water. He writes: "Beside the old priory of Commagny, a mile or two to the southwest of Moulins-Engilbert, there is a spring of St. Gervais, whither the inhabitants go in procession to obtain rain or fine weather according to the needs of the crops. In times of great drought they throw into the basin of the fountain an ancient stone image of the saint that stands in a sort of niche from which the fountain flows."

In the Paris edition of the New York Herald (August 18, 1929) we read of a drought which menaced the crops in one of the Chinese provinces. The rice crops were ruined by lack of rain, and a famine set in. The farmers, backed by the merchants who saw their business in rice endangered, planned a huge meeting for prayer to the god of rain and the god of harvest. The government frowned upon this superstitious practice on the ground that it was out of keeping with the enlightenment of modern China. However, after enduring the opposition for over a month, during which the drought grew worse, the authorities yielded, and the mammoth prayer-meeting was held. Strange to say, rain fell on the day after the meeting, and the farmers naturally ascribed the downpour to their rain god. In token of thankfulness, the people carried the image of the god through the streets.

Ancient peoples, as well as half-civilized tribes of our own day, believed that certain stones, when brought in contact with water, were potent to produce rain.

Outside the walls of Rome, in the vicinity of the temple of Mars, reposed such a stone, perhaps a hollow meteorite, called "the flowing stone" (lapis manalis). [19] When the crops were suffering from lack of rain, the pontiffs, accompanied by the magistrates and their lictors, dragged the stone into the city to the altar of Jupiter Elicius on the Aventine.

Here they drenched it with water, or if, as is generally believed, it was hollow, filled it to overflowing—a rite calculated by sympathetic magic to cause the heavens to overflow. Ovid indicates the magic nature of the rite where he represents Picus and Faunus chanting spells to induce Jupiter to come down from the sky. [20] Petronius represents women, barefoot, with flowing hair, climbing up to the Capitol to petition Jupiter for rain. The god answered their plea, and the women went home as wet as drowned rats. [21] As the setting of the Satyricon is, for the most part, in southern Italy, a Greek rite may be intended. The "flowing stone" in this rite must not be confused with the stone of the same name which, according to Festus, [22] was the gateway to the underworld. Tertullian doubtless has the same or a similar rite in mind when he says: [23] "When the sky is paralyzed and the year is rainless, barefoot processions are declared. The magistrates lay aside the purple, reverse their fasces, offer prayer, and sacrifice a victim." The fact that the magistrates doffed their purple-edged dress and the lictors reversed their fasces points to the conclusion that the rites were believed to lie outside the realm of recognized religion—within the sphere of magic.

In this rite of the aquaelicium, not only does the actual rain-making belong to the realm of magic, but that women were barefoot and had their hair streaming has magic significance as well, a point which we have noticed in our chapters on taboo. Doubtless the stone, representing the sky and not Jupiter Elicius, was at first concerned. The use of a stone to represent the sky was not unusual in Greece. Greek astronomers so employed a stone—a globe resting on a pillar. An Etruscan boundary stone was often spheroidal in shape on a rectangular base, the stone probably representing the sky. Furthermore, meteorites, having fallen from the sky, signified the sky to primitive minds and could quite easily be used to produce rain, because of the habit of incorrect application of the law of the association of ideas.

On March sixteenth and seventeenth, a solemn procession made a circuit of twenty-seven chapels called "Argei" located in various parts of the city of Rome. [24] Rush puppets, bearing the same name, and resembling bound men, were made in the chapels, where they reposed until May fourteenth or fifteenth, when the pontiffs and the generals (praetores) carried them in procession to the Sublician Bridge over the Tiber. Here the Vestals threw them into the river in the presence of the generals and the wife of the Priest of Jupiter, who was in mourning. Ovid records several explanations of the rite which were current in his day: In ancient times, two men had been sacrificed to Saturn, the god of sowing, and thrown into the Tiber; with the coming to Italy of Hercules, who substituted straw puppets for the men, the practice of throwing puppets into the river began. Another account tells how the younger generation of Romans, in order to secure the voting privilege for themselves alone, threw all men who were over sixty years of age from certain bridges, proba-bly—as we read in Festus, [25] who tells the same story—the bridges in the Plain of Mars over which the Romans passed when going to vote. This version, of course, cannot explain a rite which took place, not in the Plain of Mars, but on a bridge over the Tiber. Still another story had it that the followers of Hercules (Argivi), having established themselves in Italy, refused to travel farther with their leader. When one of them was dying, however, the longing for his native land seized him, and he gave instructions that his body should be thrown into the Tiber to be carried to his native shores. The slave who was his heir refused to carry out his master's request and threw a straw puppet into the river in place of his master.

An attempt has been made in modern times to revive the an-cient Roman explanation of this rite [26]—that the puppets represented, by substitution, a survival of the times when old men had actually been sacrificed and thrown into the Tiber, possibly to pacify the river god for the building of the bridge. We are disposed to follow

Fowler, [27] who is convinced that the rite is a case of sympathetic magic, the purpose of which is to produce rain and fertility for the crops. A comparative study of this rite with other magic rites among various peoples strengthens this conclusion.

The magic elements are clear: the straw puppets, made to look like men, were as good as men themselves in a magic rite, whether or not the rite originated in human sacrifice. Again, if the straw represented the products of the earth, the "corn spirit" as it is called, [28] the puppets, when drenched with water, were sufficient to cause rain to fall, just as the "flowing stone" when drenched with water could cause the heavens to overflow. This view is strengthened by the prominent part taken in the rite by the Vestals, who, in all their public duties, were concerned with rites to produce fertility in crops and flocks, and who, as we know, were felt to be possessed of magical powers. The procession involved purification, a magic rite in itself.

On the twenty-fifth of April, at the Festival of Robigus [29] (Robigalia), the spirit of the mildew, a suckling puppy and a sheep were slain in the city in the morning, and the entrails and the blood were carried in the afternoon by the priest of Mars, attended by worshipers clad in white, to the grove of Robigus at the fifth milestone from Rome on the Claudian Road. Here they were offered on an altar, together with unmixed wine and incense, as a burnt sacrifice to the god, with prayer to Robigus to spare the crops and to ward off harm from them. On this day, boys and men participated in foot races. Now we have record of a sacrifice of reddish puppies, offered near an otherwise unknown Puppies' Gate. From the entrails of the puppies, auguries were taken—a rite which, while it may have had an independent origin, probably was identical in historical times with the Festival of the Spirit of the Mildew. The rite was a case of homoeopathic magic—a red dog to keep off the red mildew, or, if you prefer, to bring the crops to ruddy ripeness. Ovid once, when returning to Rome from Nomentum, witnessed the ceremonies of the Festival of the Mildew, and on inquiring their purpose, received answer from the sacrificing priest that the rites were intended to keep off the destructive heat of the Dog Star. Ovid writes: [30] "This dog is set on the altar instead of the star dog, and its mere name is sufficient for it to perish." This statement is illuminating, for it clearly shows the same psychology in the sacrificing priest that we find in the savage performing a magic rite. Because the star is called "Dog" a dog in sacrifice will drive away the star and its heat—a process of homoeopathic magic.

It would seem that Robigus was a form of Mars. Tertullian connects the two in a passage [31] in which he ascribes to Numa the institution of games to Mars and Robigus. We have seen that the priest of Mars officiated at the rites of the Robigalia.

April fifteenth marked one of the most ancient rites of the Romans, the Festival of the Pregnant Cows (Fordicidia). [32] On this day, in historical times, the pontiffs sacrificed pregnant cows (called fordae or hordae) to Earth. Some of the cows were slaughtered on the Capitol for the State, and thirty others in the thirty curiae, one for each curia. The Romans themselves believed that the sacrifice was to produce fertility for the crops. Ovid says: [33] "Now the cattle are heavy with young; the earth, too, is heavy with seed. To the full earth a full victim is given." The magic element underlying the sacrifice is simply this: the cows possessed fertility, and their sacrifice to Earth transferred this fertility to the earth.

The most interesting part of the rite for our study of magic is the tearing of the calves, as yet unborn, from their mothers' wombs, under the supervision of the oldest of the Vestals. These calves were burnt by the Vestal and the ashes were preserved until the Festival of Pales on the twenty-first of April. The blood from a horse known as the October Horse, sacrificed on the Ides of October, was mixed with the ashes of the calves and with sulphur, and some of the mixture was thrown into burning bean stalks, through which man and beast leaped—a rite of purification intended to ward off hostile influence from man and beast and crops, and to induce fertility. The Vestals distributed a portion of the mixture—known as suffimen—at the altar of Vesta as a fertility charm. The ashes of the calves, having come from a prolific mother, were believed to give creative strength to the men and women who used the mixture. [34] Other magic elements in this rite—leaping, bonfires—we shall discuss in a later chapter. [35]

At the Festival of Ceres (Cerealia) on April nineteenth, foxes were let loose in the Circus Maximus with torches tied to their backs. Ovid explains [36] the custom by telling a story which he had heard from the lips of a friend at Carseoli. It appears that a boy caught a vixen fox which had been playing havoc among the chickens on his father's farm. To punish the thief, the boy wrapped her in straw and hay and set her afire. The fox managed to escape, and soon flames had seized the crops and destroyed them. This rite has puzzled scholars, and many explanations have been forthcoming. The latest is that of Frazer. [37] He believes that the burning of the fox "was intended to serve as an awful warning to other foxes not to come and poach on the farmer's fields." Doubtless here the familiar principle of similarity offers an explanation of the rite. The fox is red and hence keeps off red foxes and, in fact, anything red, mildew, for example, and fire. The firebrands attached to the wolf's tail assist in warding off the red flames which, in the dry season, would menace the crops and flocks.

Having explained and illustrated the general principles underlying magic acts, we may proceed to a study of magic acts as we find them embedded in the rites of Roman religion.

CHAPTER V
Removing Evils by Magic Acts

MAGIC ACTS in Roman religion are intended to remove the harmful effects of contact with religiously dangerous persons and things, possessing, as we say, negative mana or taboo; to ward off real or potential evil influences which have not as yet harmed the person, and to communicate to the person, by striking, some quality possessed by the striker or by the object which is used to strike. Often the same magic performance is double-acting: it wards off evil and induces good at the same time.

When man finds that he has unavoidably come in contact with some person or thing which has been found by experience to possess negative mana or taboo, he may rid himself of the evil effects of the contagion in various ways. In highly developed religions, a sacrifice is often felt to be necessary. A concubine, for instance, might not touch the temple of Juno. An ancient law with regard to this prohibition, ascribed to Numa, reads as follows: [1] "Let no kept mistress touch the temple of Juno. If she does so, let her, with streaming hair, kill and offer up a ewe lamb to Juno." Again, no graving tools were allowed in the sacred grove of the Arval Brothers; and so an atoning sacrifice of a pig and a lamb was made before the tools were taken into the grove and again after they had been removed. [2] Furthermore, rites must be repeated if a religiously dangerous person had polluted the place where they were to be celebrated. Thus, in 491 B.C., the Great Games had to be repeated because, after they had been given, it was discovered that, on the morning set for the celebration, a slave had been driven by his master through the circus where the games were to take place. [3]

Magic acts which are intended to avert evils resulting from contact with tabooed objects most commonly involve the use of purifying instruments called by the Romans februa, [4] such as water, fire, wool, the skins of sacrificial animals, laurel, pine, spelt, salt, sulphur, and any object which they used to cleanse their bodies. Evils, physical and spiritual alike, may be washed or burned away by the use of these objects. In the case of instruments of purification called februa, the object itself has the power to ward off the ill effects of contact; but there is, in almost every case, an incantation and an assisting action to bring the purifying agent in contact with the person or thing to be purified. However, it is the mysterious quality (mana) in the agent itself which has the power to avert the evil effects of contact. In the case of sticks, wands, brooms, and the like, it is primarily the action which averts the ill.

A distinction must be made at this juncture between instruments of purification (februa) on the one hand and talismans and amulets on the other. In the case of februa, as we have pointed out, there is an attendant incantation, and the object is used as an element in a magic rite; in the case of talismans and amulets, no magic rite is involved—the force is passive, so to speak; it is by inherent mana that the talisman wards off evil and the amulet induces good. It must be remembered, however, that the same object may be either februum, amulet, or talisman, depending on its purpose. If the purpose is purification from contact with tabooed persons or things, it is a februum; if it is calculated to ward off evil influences, without magic action, it is a talisman; if it is believed to induce good, it is an amulet. Wool, for example, is a februum when it is used in rites of the Lupercalia to wipe the blood from the brows of the youthful priests, for the purpose there is purification: it involves a magic act in a regular religious ceremony. However, the wool worn by the priests and by the victims may be either talisman or amulet: through its own mana, without a magic act, it wards off evil and induces good. Again, the bulla worn by the Roman boy was a talisman-amulet: it warded off evil primarily, but thereby induced good.

Most instruments of purification used in Roman religion were employed also in magic rites. In the latter, the individual is usually involved, and the object of the rite is often questionable or even evil; in religious rites, on the contrary, the general welfare is involved and the object is usually good.

We are now ready to turn to a Roman festival in which many purificatory agents are used—the Festival of Pales (Palilia). [5] This festival unquestionably antedated the founding of the city, [6] which, according to tradition, occurred on the same day as the celebration of the festival. Pales, to whom the day was sacred, was an ancient Italian shepherd divinity, of uncertain sex, worshiped on April twenty-first, in the city as well as in the country. Ovid himself had taken part in the celebration: he had with his own hands carried the ashes of the calves and the bean stalks which were used in rites of purification; and he had jumped through the fumigating fires and had been sprinkled with water from a laurel spray. Although animal sacrifice was forbidden on this day, [7] the blood from the tail and head of a horse, familiarly known as the October Horse, which had been sacrificed on October fifteenth, was mixed with sulphur and with bean stalks and with the ashes of the unborn calves which had been sacrificed at the Festival of the Pregnant Cows (Fordicidia) on April fifteenth. This mixture was distributed at the Festival of Pales as a fertility charm.

On the morning of the festival, the shepherds ceremonially swept their folds with a broom and sprinkled both sheep and folds with purificatory water. They adorned the folds with laurel sprays and fumigated the sheep with sulphur, while male olives, pine, and savines were thrown into the fire, presumably on the hearth of the farmhouse. These would crackle if the omens were favorable. Baskets of millet, millet cakes, and milk were offered to Pales, whose wooden statue, standing near the farmhouse, seems to have been splashed with milk. A feast followed in which shepherds and god took part. The shepherds then prayed to Pales to keep away evil influences—wolves, disease, hunger—and to bring good influences to bear—water, food, health to man and to flocks; they repeated the prayer four times, facing the East, while they cleansed their hands in fresh dew. The people drank wine boiled down until it was thick and then mixed with milk. After this, the farmer, his family, and his flocks leaped through bonfires made of straw, a rite which, as they believed, would make women prolific. The worshipers, eating and drinking, lay about on the grass.

We have noted in this rite many of the purifying instruments mentioned by Ovid under the name februa. Water is used to cleanse, fire to burn away evil influences. Sulphur is burned as a fumigating agent for flocks and men. There has also been a ceremonial sweeping of the folds. Some notion of spiritual cleansing may be associated with the purificatory objects here used, as well as with the ceremonial sweeping. The significance of these various februa and of the magic sweeping we shall presently consider in detail.

Rites similar to or almost identical with those of the Festival of Pales have survived to our day in various parts of the world. Frazer writes: [8]

"In eastern Europe many analogous rites have been performed down to recent times, and probably still are performed, for the same purpose, by shepherds and herdsmen on St. George's Day, the twenty-third of April, only two days after the Parilia, with which they may well be connected by descent from a common festival observed by pastoral Aryan peoples in spring. The ceremonies appear to be mainly designed to guard the flocks and herds against wolves and witches. . . ."

Removing the Evil Effects of Dangerous Contact by Washing and Burning

Among all peoples, water and fire are common instruments for removing the harmful effects of contact with persons or things which, as they believe, possess a mysterious power to harm. Inasmuch as they find in everyday life that water can cleanse their household utensils and their bodies, they believe, by a curious twist in thinking, that it can cleanse them of the uncanny contagion of those persons and things which are, as we say, taboo.

We shall give a few examples of this use of water. First, an instance of its power to cleanse a stranger of the influences dangerous to a Roman. A Sabine, on one occasion, presented himself at the temple of Diana in Rome with a prodigiously large heifer, intending to sacrifice it to the goddess. Now soothsayers had prophesied that the state whose citizen should offer that particular heifer to Diana would possess the supreme power in Italy. The Roman priest, aware of the prophecy, insisted that the Sabine—a stranger and hence religiously dangerous—bathe in a running stream as the Roman ritual demanded. While the Sabine was thus occupied, the priest sacrificed the heifer to the goddess. [9] Again, corpses and death, in all ages, have been considered dangerous, and the person who has come in contact with them needs purification. Thus persons who attended a Roman funeral must wash their hands in pure water before performing the last rites for the dead, and on returning must be sprinkled with water and walk over fire to remove the contagion of death. [10]

AEneas, we recall, refused to touch his home gods until he had removed the blood of battle from his hands. [11] Again, before Claudia Quinta laid hold of the cable of the ship bearing the Great Mother and forced it to move, thus proving her chastity, she dipped her hands in the Tiber and three times sprinkled her head with holy water. [12] And at the Festival of Pales, the farmer sprinkled the ground and, after prayer to the divinity, washed his hands in pure spring water. [13] Sprinkling, in such cases as these, seems to be a survival of an earlier ceremony of washing, just as in Christian sects sprinkling at a christening ceremony is a survival of an earlier immersion.

Water was commonly used in magic rites also. The witch Sagana, in Horace's fifth Epode, sprinkled with water from Lake Avernus the house in which she and two other witches were making preparations to murder a boy to secure his marrow for magic purposes. [14] One recalls the rites in which Dido (feigning thus to destroy AEneas by magic) sprinkled on the pyre pretended waters from Avernus. [15] Again, in certain rites described by Ovid which were believed to have the power to ward off evil influences from a baby, the witch sprinkled the entrance of the house with water containing a drug. [16]

Fire, like water, is regularly used to remove the harmful effects of contact with persons and things which are taboo and for driving away evils of all sorts, whether spiritual or physical. Thus, as we have seen, when a person returned from a funeral, he had to walk over fire to remove the contagion of death-a rite usually called "the fire walk." [17]

A vigorous description of purificatory rites which later Romans used after contact with a foreigner is found in a late writer. [18] The rites are intended to rid a person of the evil influences of such dangerous contact. The priest whirls lustral torches of blazing pungent sulphur and bitumen about the person to be purified; he sprinkles sacred waters and grasses which have the power to rout evil influences. With his hands turned backward he hurls torches to the south. These are to carry off with them all the spells which have been cast upon the sick. The poet, to be sure, pictures the city of Rome as the body to be purified (from contact with Alaric) ; but the rites are doubtless true to current practice, otherwise there would be no point to the figure.

Not only sulphur but other combustible substances were used as purifying agents. A witch, for example, purified Tibullus from the harmful effects of magic by using pine torches. [19] Such torches, we know, were carried in procession from the house of the bride to that of the bridegroom. [20] Ovid once heard a flamen's wife asking for instruments of purification, and a spray of pine was handed to her. [21] In most magic rites pine torches are used along with sulphur and laurel and other purifying agents. [22] In the case of purification by laurel, the person to be purified was sprinkled with water from a laurel spray. [23] The soldiers who followed the general's car in a triumphal procession wore a laurel garland that they might enter the city with the stain of blood removed, and to ward off the ghosts of the slain enemies. [24] This is a talismanic use of laurel. The war-herald who accompanied the Roman army took with him for purifying purposes certain sacred greens—in all likelihood the modern vervain which is commonly used in magic rites. [25] In the rite of treaty-making between the Romans and the Albans, prior to the contest between the Horatii and the Curiatii, the fetial took pure vervain and touched the head of the spokesman (pater patratus) of the Roman side. The words of the treaty, which Livy felt were not worth quoting, were in verse, in keeping with the magic character of the rite. [26]

Removing Evils by Sweeping and Striking

In Roman religious rites, various instruments for sweeping and strik-ing were used to drive away evils of all sorts, whether physical or spiritual. For this purpose the Romans used branches of certain trees, wands, lashes, brooms and besoms. To take an example: after a dead body had been carried out for burial at Rome, scruples de-manded that the house be swept out ceremonially. Festus writes as follows [27] about the person who performed the rite: "Everriator (the one who sweeps out) is the name given to the person who, having by law received an inheritance, is bound to perform due rites to the dead. If he fails to do so, or if there is any interference in this rite, he shall atone with his life. This name is derived from the process of sweeping out." Ovid mentions the rite: [28] "After houses have been swept out, the objects of purification which the lictor takes—parched spelt and salt—are called februa." Here, then, we have a magic cere-mony performed, either by a State official—a lictor who customarily assisted the Priest of Jupiter—or, as is implied in what Festus writes, by the heir of the deceased. It is our purpose here to note that there is a ceremonial sweeping of the house with a particular kind of broom, the purpose of which, as Frazer suggests [29] (supporting his belief with parallels from many lands), was to sweep out the ghosts of the deceased, and also, we may add, to sweep out the evils which had caused his death. Spelt and salt were regularly used in magic rites of purification and as offerings to the spirits of the dead; hence the appropriateness of their use here. [30]

Our second illustration of magic sweeping comes from St.

Augustine, who describes [31] the danger surrounding the mother and her new-born child—the superstition that they were liable to be tormented by evil spirits from the woodland (Silvanus, as the later Romans believed) until a curious ceremony was performed. We have had occasion to quote the passage before; but its appropriateness to the present subject leads us to give it again and to discuss it a little more fully.

"After the birth of the child, three protecting divinities are summoned lest the god Silvanus enter during the night and harass mother and child; and to give tokens of those guardian divinities three men by night surround the threshold of the house and first strike it with an ax and a pestle; then they sweep it off with a broom, that, by giving these signs of worship, the god Silvanus may be kept from entering. For trees are not cut nor pruned without iron; nor is spelt powdered without a pestle; nor is grain piled up without a broom. Now from these three objects are named three divinities: Intercidona from the intercisio of the ax; Pilumnus from the pilum; Deverra from the 'sweeping' (verrere) of the broom; and by the protection of these divinities new-born babes are preserved against the violence of Silvanus."

Needless to say, this rite fairly teems with magic. The objects used in it are talismanic: they are possessed of mana potent to drive away evil influences. The iron of the ax and the iron tip of the pestle in themselves have power to drive away baleful forces; and this is assisted by the power of the ax to kill with its sharp edge. The striking with the pestle and the ceremonial sweeping are familiar magic acts of aversion.

We have already had occasion to describe the Festival of Pales. [32] We must notice here again, however, that the shepherds on the morning of the festival ceremonially swept their folds to drive away dangerous forces.

We conclude our description of ceremonial sweeping with an account of the cleansing of the temple of Vesta on the fifteenth of June. The muck (stercus) thus swept out was carried up the Capitoline Hill to an alley shut off by a gate called the Muck Gate (Porta Stercoria), where it was buried. [33] The other sweepings (purgamina) from the temple were thrown into the Tiber. [34] The day was a holiday until after the ceremony was completed. Frazer (following Wissowa) has assumed [35] that the sweepings mentioned by Ovid and the muck recorded in Festus and in Varro were one and the same thing; and he has conjectured that these were placed in a depository on the Capitoline Hill and were subsequently dumped into the Tiber. Now the word purgamina in Latin signifies "sweepings," but it does not necessarily mean "muck." Purgamina is commonly used of sweepings in magic rites which are calculated to drive away evil spirits. Thus, in my opinion, stercus and purgamina were two different things. The sweeping of the temple of Vesta may be a survival of the primitive days when the daughters of the family actually swept out the rude hut. [36] The sweeping, then, in historical times would be a ritualistic survival of this act.

Whipping and striking are favorite ways of driving evils out of persons and things, and thereby allowing good influences to take their place. For example, when a Vestal in Rome had committed an offense against the proprieties of her order, the chief Priest whipped her, not only to punish her, but to drive out the evil influences which caused her wrongdoing. [37]

We shall conclude this part of our study with accounts of two festivals in which rites of magic whipping had a prominent place: the Lupercalia and the Festival of the Nones of the Goat (Nonae Caprotinae).

To discuss the various interpretations of the Lupercalia would lead us too far afield. [38] We are concerned here primarily with its magic elements and more especially with the rite of ceremonial whipping contained in it.

One of the most revered spots in the city of Rome in ancient days was the cave at the base of the Palatine Hill called the Lupercal, with the sacred fig tree hard by, under whose shadow, as the story went, a she-wolf suckled Remus and Romulus. Here, on February fifteenth, a goat and a dog, together with certain salt cakes baked by the Vestals, were sacrificed, whether to Lupercus, Faunus, Inuus, or Juno is problematic. Justin Martyr mentions [39] an image of Lupercus which stood in the Lupercal, nude save for a girdle of goatskin. There seems to be no good reason for believing that this statue represented a god Lupercus: it may well have represented one of the priests; and, inasmuch as the rites of the Lupercalia are very old and have magic significance, no god need be involved at all. Because of the curious medley of rites in the festival, the ancients assigned it to various divinities, not realizing that no god was necessary.

A bloody knife, fresh from the sacrifice, was smeared across the brows of two youths of aristocratic families, probably leaders of two colleges of priests called Luperci. The blood was wiped off with wool which had been dipped in milk, and the youths were compelled to laugh. Blood, we know, was commonly used in magic rites; and goats, too, often had a place in these rites. The blood of a goat, for example, was believed to possess the power to break adamant. By the principles of magic, the blood of the goat and the dog would, in itself, be sufficient to drive away evil—in this case, probably wolves at first and then, because of the wolf's connection with Mars, all the evil influences centered in that god. But it would be easier to explain the rite's connection with wolf aversion if the actual sacrifice were a wolf. Perhaps wolves were originally sacrificed, and when these dangerous creatures became less available for sacrificial purposes, dogs were substituted for them. Such substitutions are easy for primitive peoples. Servius, for instance, writes: [40] "In sacrifice, likenesses are accepted for realities. Hence, when animals which are difficult to find must be sacrificed, they are made of bread or of wax and are accepted as the real victims." Certainly in the rites of the Lupercalia the smiling of the youths smacks of the grinning of wolves, and so, by the principle of similarity, the Luperci became wolves so far as magic was concerned, and thus originally kept off wolves.

The rite which ensued is of particular interest at this point. The Luperci, clad only in a magic girdle made of the skins of the sacrificial goats, made a purificatory circuit of the city, beginning at the Lupercal, forming as they ran a magic circle, the object of which was to keep off evil influences—here again, no doubt, originally wolves—from the sheepfold of the primitive Palatine settlement. As the youths ran, they smote the hands of any women who placed themselves in their path. There seems to have been no incantation or prayer accompanying this rite. We know that lashings of this sort were believed, among other peoples, to expel evil influences of all sorts and to stir up the reproductive powers; and the Romans, in historical times, believed that this was the object of the lashings at the Lupercalia. The fertility of the goat was by some mysterious force transferred to the women through this contact. Inasmuch, too, as primitive peoples closely associate fertility in women with fertility in crops, the rites may have been intended to promote productiveness of the soil as well. [41]

Our final festival—the Festival of the Nones of the Goat [42]—occurred on July seventh, the day on which, according to tradition, Romulus disappeared at the Goat's Marsh in the Plain of Mars (Campus Martius). On this day slave women, dressed in their mistresses' clothes, ran about in play, scoffing at passers-by and engaging in a kind of sham fight in which they cast stones at one another. They feasted and drank under fig-tree boughs in the Plain of Mars and, along with their mistresses, cut sprays from the sacred fig tree and sacrificed them and their milky juice to Juno of the Goat. Now the fig is purgative, and such purgatives were ceremonially used by the ancients as cathartics to expel evil influences and hence to induce good. The resemblance of the sap of the fig to milk and the fact that the sacrifice, in historical times, was made to the especial goddess of mothers, make the object of the rite fairly sure. The male fig communicates its richness to the divinity who, in turn, communicates it to the women. Moreover, we have the curious statement recorded in Varro [43] about this festival: "They use the switch from the (male) wild fig-tree." While we are not told exactly what use was made of it, it is reasonable to suppose that the women lashed one another with it and thus transferred by magic the fertility of the fig to themselves, driving out at the same time any influences detrimental to reproduction. We have record of similar lashings with wild fig switches at the Thargelia in Athens in the curious rite of riddance by two scapegoats called pharmakoi. [44]

Originally these rites may have had some connection with the fertilization, by the aid of insects, of the female cultivated fig tree by the pollen of the male fig, a process which the ancients sought to further, about this season of the year, by placing strips of the fruit of the wild fig among the boughs of the cultivated variety. [45] The throwing of stones at one another by the maidservants also shows this to be a fertility rite. There was a similar throwing of stones in the temple of Hippolytus at Troezen at the festival of the two divinities Damia and Auxesis, both fertility deities.

Keeping Away Evils by Drawing a Magic Circle

The describing of a circle about the person or thing to be protected was usual in magic rites. [46] Thus magic circles could protect one against snakes. [47] The Roman ceremonial drawing of circles by processions about persons and things had its origin in such a belief. We have record of several magic processions among the Romans. Thus, in founding towns, they employed an Etruscan rite. [48] On an auspicious day, they yoked a white bull and a white cow to a plough with a bronze share. The ploughman, with his left side turned toward the proposed town, drove to the left, with the bull on the outside and the cow on the inside. Thus he traced a furrow around the city, marking out the line of the proposed wall and being careful that the upturned earth should fall inwards, toward the left and the town. The furrow, however, was not unbroken, for wherever a gate was to be built, the share was removed and the plough was lifted from the ground. The line thus traced—known as the pomerium—was considered sacred; but such spots as were intended for gates were not so considered, because dangerous persons—strangers, enemies, soldiers contaminated by death and blood—had to pass through. Moreover, dead bodies must go through the gates, and these would contaminate anything sacred. The magic circle so described was believed to be effective in keeping away evil influences of all sorts, demons, witches, diseases, plagues, and the like. The pomerium therefore constituted a magic line of demarcation between the sacred and the profane. Hence it was that the Romans would ordinarily not allow foreign gods within the sacred line, and generals and their armies had to be purified before entering the city. The use of bronze for the ploughshare has already been discussed. [49] The Romans usually considered the left auspicious. Hence the ploughman turned up the clods of earth to the left and drove his plough to the left. There was a yearly dramatization of this original rite called the amburbium, but unfortunately we know no more about the rite than that there was a procession about the city and that there was a sacrificial victim. [50]

The lustration of the farm, usually held in May, took the form of a procession around its bounds, consisting of a pig, a sheep, and a bull (suovetaurilia), driven by a throng of people wearing garlands, chanting and waving olive branches. The procession made a circuit of the farm three times, at the conclusion of which the sacrifice of the suovetaurilia was made to Mars, with an offering of wine, and prayer to Janus and Jupiter. We translate Cato's description of the rite: [51]

"The cultivated land should be purified as follows: Order the suovetaurilia to be driven around. . . . First pray to Janus and to Jupiter, with offering of wine, and (then) say thus: 'Father Mars I pray and entreat thee to be favorable and propitious to me, my home, and my slaves (familia); and with this aim I have ordered the suovetaurilia to be driven around my arable field, land, and farm, that thou mayest ward off, debar, and keep away from us diseases, seen and unseen, dearth, devastation, disasters, inclement weather; and that thou mayest permit the products, grain, vineyards, and shrubbery to come to full growth and prove a success; and that thou mayest keep the shepherds and their flocks safe, and grant good health and strength to me, my home, and my slaves; and to this end, as I have stated it—the purification and lustration of my farm, land, and cultivated field-be thou strengthened by this sacrifice of the suckling suovetaurilia.'"

Then a cake is sacrificed. Cato continues: "When you sacrifice the pig, lamb, and calf, you must say this: 'To this end, be thou strengthened by the sacrifice of the suovetaurilia.'" If the sacrifice is not successful, another is made, with the following prayer: "'Father Mars, if in anything thou hast not been satisfied with this sacrifice of the suckling suovetaurilia, I make atonement with this suovetaurilia.'"

If, in the case of one or more victims, there has been doubt whether Mars was satisfied or not, a pig is sacrificed, with these words: "'Father Mars, because, in the case of the pig offered, satisfaction has not been given to thee, I make atonement to thee with this pig.'" The words of the prayer to be made to Janus, the god of the doorway, and to Jupiter, the god of the sky, are not given—probably because the necessity of ridding the farm of the evil influences which centered in Mars was more compelling.

There are three elements in the prayer to Mars: first, a petition that Mars ward off evil influences, a power which he possesses by reason of the fact that he is the source of these influences; [52] second, a petition that he bring good influences to bear upon the farm; and, third, in some mystic way the god is to receive strength to act by partaking of the sacrifice. [53] The god Mars addressed in these formulae is, of course, a fully developed god, represented in the ritual of the State as the god of war; but the ritual and the prayers hark back to a more primitive period, when man made no distinction between himself and the things and forces with which he found himself beleaguered in his struggle with nature. The primitive farmer probably addressed, not a god, but disease, dearth, and the rest, as real spirits, and, being incapable, as it seems, of conceiving a force as emanating from something unlike himself, he came gradually to ascribe personality to the spirits, who were to be warded off by what was in all probability a charm, the forerunner of these prayers in Cato. This was followed by a gradual accumulation of all the hostile spirits into one great hostile spirit, Mars, the spirit, powerful for ill, who dwelt in the regions beyond the bounds of the farm, and who must be induced to keep away. [54]

But the lustration, while it passed through this animistic stage before it became connected with Mars, Janus, and Jupiter, had its origin further back in the age of magic. It was originally a process of marking off the sacred from the profane by a magic circle formed by the slow procession from point to point on a Roman farm. In the procession were carried, or driven, the sacred animals, the pig, the sheep, and the bull. The animals originally possessed sufficient mana—in this case their productivity—to communicate it to the fields and flocks. No god or spirit was at first concerned in the rite. A charm, in the form of a command, accompanied the tracing of the magic circle, and this was sufficient to ward off evils.

Removing Evils by Dancing: The Scapegoat

Dancing played a prominent part in ancient Roman rites and seems to involve principles of sympathetic magic. On the first of March began a series of processions lasting throughout the whole month, in which twenty-four priests of Mars, called Leapers (Salii), clad in armor of bronze, each carrying in his right hand a staff and in his left a shield, marched in procession through the city, visiting certain important spots such as the Forum and the Capitol. They danced in solemn rhythm, chanting their ancient hymn and beating their shields with their staffs. On the fourteenth of the month, a man called Mamurius Veturius, clad in the skins of a goat, was beaten with the staffs and driven from the city. [55] Frazer has gathered [56] many parallels to these rites in which savages, in warlike dances, brandish swords, fire off muskets, and beat drums in order to drive away spirits hostile to crops. It would seem that such rites and, by analogy, those of the Leapers of Mars, involve principles of sympathetic magic: the crops will grow as high as the worshipers can leap; the striking, too, drives away hostile demons of all sorts. The smiting of the scapegoat—probably representing Mars, the accumulated hostile spirits of the farm and, later, of the city—transferred to him the evils which were harmful to crops and flocks and men, and these were carried away when the scapegoat was driven out.

In historical times, certain Leaping Maidens, dressed exactly like the Leapers, and performing some, if not all, of the functions of their male colleagues, were hired to take part in the rites. [57] It has been suggested that originally they may have been priestesses of Mars, with important functions. [58]

Servius records [59] a curious incident which illustrates the power of dancing to avert the evil effects of desecrating the sacred games. While the games of Apollo were in progress, news reached the city that Hannibal was making an attack near one of the gates. Everyone took up arms to repel the enemy. On returning home, however, they were seized by dread of the evil consequences of their having interrupted the sacred games. Noticing an old man dancing in the Circus, they inquired the reason for his action. He replied: "I have not interrupted my dancing." There are several possible explanations. Servius believes that the Roman proverb "The State is safe while the old man dances" originated in this event; and inasmuch as he tells the story apropos of a line of Vergil which mentions an interruption in sacred rites, he must feel that the dancing in some way atoned for the interrupted rites of Apollo. It may be possible, however, that his dance was imitative of war actions, in which case he would help the Romans by sympathetic magic; or he may have danced in order thus to keep the games of Apollo in progress.

To summarize: We have noticed in this chapter that magic acts in Roman religion may be divided, according to their objects, into three classes: those which are calculated to remove the baleful effects of actual contact with persons and things which have, in the past, been found to be uncannily dangerous to man; those which are intended to keep off potential evils, whether physical or spiritual; and, finally, those which are intended to communicate to the person struck some quality possessed by the striker or by the object used to strike. Such magic rites are often double-acting; they ward off evils and induce good at the same time.

The evil effects of contact with dangerous persons or things may be removed in several ways: in developed religions, where some notion of a personal god is present, sacrifice may be necessary, or a whole rite may have to be repeated. Most magic acts, however, involve the use of certain instruments of purification—called februa by the Romans—such as fire, water, wool, and the like. By means of these, evils both physical and spiritual are washed or burned away. Some mysterious power to ward off evil is believed to be present in these objects: the magic act is purely secondary. In the case of sticks, wands, and besoms, however, it is primarily the action, often accompanied by an incantation, which averts the ill. All such instruments of purification are used both in magic and in religious rites among ancient peoples and among savages of to-day. In the case of magic rites, the individual is concerned; in religion the common good is involved.

We have seen, too, that all magic instruments of purification were used in the Roman State festivals; that rites similar to those of old Rome are occasionally to be found among modern peoples—a fact which points to a common origin for such festivals.

We have seen, further, that water and fire are commonly used in religious and in magic rites to wash and to burn away evils. Early man, knowing that water cleansed his body and his household vessels, thought that it could wash away the contagion of things which he felt to be dangerous to him. Such is the curious reasoning of savages.

Again, he saw that fire refined the dross from metal, so why should it not burn away evils which were actually harming him and keep off evils which might harm him in the future? Thus we have ceremonial leapings through bonfires and walking over hot coals. These fires, too, may have been felt as setting up barriers between the living and the dead. Sulphur, because of its real disinfectant properties and because of its fiery nature, is particularly potent in rites of purification.

Evils, as we have shown, can also be driven away by striking and by sweeping, rites which have parallels among all peoples. Early man could sweep the filth from his hovel, so why could he not sweep out the spirit of the dead man? Often, as we have noticed, such ceremonies are believed to keep away the hostile spirits of the dead, or to drive away evil influences which might interfere with childbearing, or to communicate, by contact through lashings, the fertility of some fruitful object, an animal or a tree, for example.

We have seen that evils of all sorts can be kept away by tracing a magic line about them. This protecting rite is often assisted by driving in the procession animals whose fertility is communicated to the crops.

And, finally, rites of dancing seem to have a sympathetic connection with the crops: these will grow as high as the dancers can leap. In such rites magic striking is also found.

CHAPTER VI
Incantation and Prayer

A STUDY of the Roman prayers which have come down to us, whether they be found in their original integrity as in the Carmen Saliare, the Carmen Arvale, the prayer of the Umbrian Attiedii, those of the farmer recorded by Cato in his De Agricultura; or whether, like those embedded in the Fasti of Ovid, they have been modified by the poets to meet the requirements of meter—all will, we believe, show that they are, in their essential nature, magic incantations. Our problem is not whether prayer has developed from incantation or whether a spell is a degenerated prayer. [1] It would seem, after a detailed study of a large number of Roman prayers, that these always retained some of the characteristics of an incantation; and if there is any difference between the two it lies chiefly not in the prayer or incantation as such, but in the mental attitude of the person toward the object of his incantation or prayer, and in the consequent change in the tone and, in a limited degree, in the form of the incantation.

It will be necessary at the outset to define what we mean by "incantation." An incantation is a command (or, rarely, a wish), usually chanted, addressed to the subject of the magic rite. [2] The shepherdess in the song of Alphesiboeus in Vergil's eighth Eclogue repeats nine times the words "Lead Daphnis home from the city, my charms, lead Daphnis home." In certain rites of riddance described by Ovid [3] a child is to be protected by an incantation and a magic act. The protection is commanded in these words: "Birds of the night, spare the entrails of the boy." Such incantations containing a command are found commonly in private magic, and traces of their influence may be seen in the Roman State religion. If the spell was intended to harm a person, the State could interfere to protect him. [4] For instance, it was not unusual for a farmer whose crops had failed to accuse another of having, by a spell (carmen), lured the crops away. Tibullus, in a poem [5] in which he complains that an old beldame has bewitched Marathus, takes the opportunity to recount various feats of witches, such as transferring crops from one field to another. Similarly, Pliny the Elder records [6] that a certain freedman, Furius, by using better implements and better methods than his neighbor, was able to obtain richer crops from a smaller strip of land. A neighbor haled Furius before the tribes and accused him of having bewitched his field. But when they saw his sturdy slaves and his implements of witchcraft—hoes, rakes, and ploughs—they acquitted him.

The Romans of later days restricted the use of the term carmina to slander and libel, giving the names dirae and defixiones to such spells as we have just mentioned.

The tendency of the growing mind of early man was to personify the object addressed; and along with this tendency came another—to assign a spirit to the object (animism), causing the spell to change its character somewhat. But, as we have suggested, the difference between a spell and a prayer lies not so much in any inherent change in the nature of either as in a shift in the attitude of mind toward the object to be influenced and in the consequent alteration in the tone of the prayer. In magic the process is purely mechanical. The person performing the rite wills a certain effect which is bound to ensue if the magic act and the incantation have been flawless. The volition lies with the person. In the case of prayer, however, the worshiper addresses a divinity, all-powerful in his sphere, whose will he must win just as he would win the will of a person. Here, then, lies the fundamental difference between incantation and prayer, so far, at least, as the mental attitude of the person is concerned: in the incantation the will of the person, in the prayer the will of the divinity, determines the effect. Furthermore, when with the passing of the years ancient religions degenerated into mere forms without meaning, and the notion of the divinity involved in the rite was lost, the prayer once more took on the nature of a spell.

We have a clear illustration of this degenerative tendency in the case of the curious goddess Carna who in ancient times had control over the vital organs of the human being. Carna was a recognized divinity of the Roman State religion; but in the popular religio she was considered a witch. The goddess has survived in modern Tuscany where she is known as Carradora, a kindly spirit with substantially the same functions as the ancient Carna. [7]

We shall attempt in this chapter to show that a Roman prayer and a Roman incantation had six elements in common and that in only one essential point were they different. In order to do this we must first notice the characteristics of a Roman incantation and then see whether these characteristics are to be found in the Roman prayer.

As characteristics of the Roman incantation we may mention

the following: (1) It was in the form of a command; (2) it was chanted; (3) it was uttered in an undervoice; (4) in order to be effective it must be repeated; (5) the wording of the incantation must be exact; (6) the usual purpose of the incantation was secretly to secure evil ends; (7) no god was involved in the incantation.

Prayer a Command

In magic rites, the incantation is almost always in the form of a command. Thus a charm for driving away gout reads: [8] "Away, away from my feet and from all my limbs, gout and every muscular pain." We have seen in the rites of Crane, the witch who possessed the power to keep off bloodsucking vampires, that these baleful creatures are addressed in the form of a command. [9] This direct address in the form of a command is found in rites of the State religion. At the Festival of the Spirit of the Mildew (Robigalia), the Priest of Mars commands Robigus to spare the young blades of grain. [10] Again, the shady merchant who desired to rid himself and his wares of evils attending a questionable deal commanded the waters of the Spring of Mercury to wash away his past perjuries. [11] In the rites of treaty-making preserved by Livy [12] the formula begins with a command: "Hear, Jupiter, hear, spokesman of the Alban People, hear, Alban People." In declaring war, the fetial began: [13] "Hear, Jupiter, and thou, Janus Quirinus, and all ye gods celestial and terrestrial and ye gods infernal, hear." Romulus in vowing a temple to Jupiter prayed: "But do thou, father of gods and men, at least keep the enemy from here, take away terror from the Romans, and stay their foul flight." [14]

Prayers Chanted

That incantations were chanted is a matter of common observance and scarcely needs illustration. That the word carmen means "song" is evidence of this. For example, in magic rites, the purpose of which was to induce a dislocated or broken bone to come together, the incantation was sung (cantare). [15] Again, a witch composed a charm for Tibullus, to be chanted three times, after which he had to spit; then Delia's husband would believe gossip about other lovers of Delia, but not about her and Tibullus. [16]

The two oldest prayers of the Romans which we possess—the Carmen Arvale and the Carmen Saliare—were both chanted. Livy writes [17] that "the leaping priests went through the city chanting their hymns." There is reason to believe that the old prayers which Cato has preserved for us in his treatise on agriculture were originally in metrical form; but in the directions given to the worshiper the verb dicito, and not cantato, precedes the prayer, showing that, in Cato's time at least, such prayers were "spoken" rather than "sung." However, these prayers, even in the form in which they are found in Cato, are predominantly spondaic, in keeping with the slow movement of the chant and with the solemn religious character of the rites. In ceremonies intended to bring thunderbolts down from the sky, incantations were used. [18]

Prayers Uttered in an Undervoice

Normally prayers were uttered aloud by the Romans. But we have reason to believe that at times they were chanted in an undervoice. [19] We know that magic rites were commonly accompanied by an incantation which was either sung almost inaudibly or muttered. [20] The prayer of the Fratres Attiedii at Iguvium was so repeated, as were the prayers recorded in Cato. Cicero definitely states that men pray silently to the gods, but he does not tell us the sort of prayers thus offered. [21] Horace, however, sheds some light on the question where he satirizes the man whom the people believe to be good, who sacrifices a pig or an ox and cries to Janus and to Apollo that all may hear, but in an undervoice prays to Laverna, the goddess of theft, that he may be able to deceive his fellows. [22] In the country festival described by Tibullus, [23] the worshiper is bidden to call upon the god audibly for the flocks but in undertones for himself. Juvenal represents [24] a mother praying in an undervoice for beauty for her sons but in louder tones for the same gift for her daughters. Persius complains [25] that his fellows petitioned aloud in the temples for a sound mind and an honorable name, but inaudibly for the death of a relative or the finding of treasure. Seneca laments [26] the fact that men in their madness whisper the vilest prayers to the gods. Finally, the Chief Priest, while lashing an errant Vestal, prayed inaudibly. [27] It seems, then, that prayers were normally uttered aloud; but when a worshiper wanted to pray for evil (as would be the case also in a magic rite) he uttered his prayers so that no one but the god could hear.

The fact that people prayed for things of which they were ashamed may explain why they whispered their prayers; but it will not explain why the priests mumbled their prayers. The reason probably lies in the fact that they were of magical significance, and if they reached the ears of the unholy or the stranger

they might prove dangerous. Thus Ovid informs us [28] that it was considered impious for one to know the charms and arts by which Jupiter was drawn down from the sky. That the priests repeated their prayers inaudibly is shown by a passage in Ovid [29] where the poet bids the reader stand at the side of the priest officiating at the Carmentalia; by keeping thus close, he will hear the priest mutter two names not before known to him, referring to Porrima and Postverta, two goddesses who had control over the manner of birth of the child, whether head or foot foremost.

Prayers Repeated

Again, repetition characterized the magic incantation. For instance, the incantation of the lover in Vergil's eighth Eclogue, already referred to, was repeated nine times; the incantation which the witch formulated for Tibullus had to be uttered three times. [30] At the conclusion of the prayer to Pales we read the words: [31] "With these words the goddess must be appeased. So do you, facing the east, utter them four times. . . ." The verses of the Carmen Saliare were each chanted three times, as the Leaping Priests of Mars danced in threefold measure. Fowler, who on the whole is not inclined to identify spell and prayer, writes [32] that the verses "seem certainly to belong rather to the region of magic than of religion proper." Repetition was also characteristic of the Carmen Arvale and the prayer of the Fratres Attiedii.

Exactness in Naming the God and in the Wording of the Prayer

To the savage mind, merely mentioning the name of the person whose will was to be influenced was sufficient to work a spell. It was necessary for the name to be correct; and from this habit of the age of magic arose the scrupulous exactness with which the Romans addressed their divinities. If the divinity had several names, the worshiper would address him by them all. Horace, for example, invokes Ilithyia (Diana) to protect mothers and adds, "whether you prefer to be addressed as Lucina or as Genitalis." [33] Again, Horace bids Father Matutinus begin his song; but he adds cautiously, "or, if you prefer the name, Janus." [34] Lucius in Apuleius' Metamorphoses [35] addresses the Queen of Heaven as Ceres, Venus, the sister of Phoebus, Proserpina, or "by whatever name, with whatever rite, in whatever appearance it is right to invoke thee." In the formula of devotio prescribed in Macrobius we read: [36] "Dis Pater, or by whatever name it is right to address thee ..." Again, in Servius, we read [37] that the pontiffs prayed: "Jupiter Optimus Maximus, or by whatever name you wish to be addressed." Finally, if the sex of the divinity was unknown, they would add "whether god or goddess, male or female." [38]

Thus the sex of Pales and Pomonus (Pomona) was indeterminate.

Not only was it necessary for the divinity to be properly addressed, but the prayer had to be uttered exactly as prescribed for the sacrifice involved; if there was a mistake in the wording, the whole rite had to be repeated or an atoning sacrifice had to be made. [39] We learn from the accounts of the Fratres Attiedii that if the brethren made an error in the prayer they had to repeat it. Juvenal represents [40] a woman standing before an altar with veiled head praying that her paramour may win a prize for his lyre-playing. The words she utters are dictata—repeated after the priest.

Prayers for Ill

Magic acts were more often calculated to do harm than good. Such magic practices were rampant as early as 450 B.C., as is evidenced by the provisions against them in the Laws of the Twelve Tables. Rome thus officially looked with disfavor upon magic intended to harm, although magic principles of similarity and contact were to be found in almost every rite of the Romans. Servius states the attitude of a much later generation of Romans toward the art when he writes: "While the Romans adopted many rites, they always condemned magic, for it was considered a base art." [41]

We shall give a few examples of prayers for evil, gathered from various Latin authors. Catullus prays to the gods to inflict evil upon one who has harmed his friends. [42] Vergil offers us three illustrations of prayers for evil—at least from our point of view. As the body of his son lies at his feet, slain by the sword of Pyrrhus, Priam prays [43] the gods to bring a like fate upon the murderer. Evander invokes [44] the gods that the murders and other high-handed acts of the tyrant Mezentius be visited in kind upon the Etruscans themselves. Ascanius, before entering into combat with Remulus, calls [45] upon Jupiter to aid him. In return for the god's assistance Ascanius will offer sacrifice at his altar. We have already seen how the Roman of Horace's day would pray for success in theft and that his sins and cheadngs might be cloaked. Propertius, like many of his fellow Romans, was quite willing to pray for evil. When, for example, a Roman praetor has displaced him in Cynthia's favor, Propertius prays: "But do you now, Venus, aid me in my grief, that he (the praetor) may destroy himself through his persistent lechery." [46]

The story is told in Velleius [47] that Merula, who, before Cinna's arrival in Rome, had abdicated his office as consul, having opened his veins with suicidal intent, implored the gods to vent their wrath on Cinna and his party, a petition which might well have been made in the form of an incantation. In Juvenal's satires we have many instances of prayers offered to the gods for questionable ends: riches, the largest money chest in the whole city, beauty for one's sons, a prize for lyre-playing at the Capitoline Games. [48] Petronius laments [49] the fact that because of the degeneracy of the times the people pray, not for eloquence or the blessings of philosophy, but for the death of a rich neighbor or the unearthing of buried treasure. Persius, like Juvenal, was wholly out of sympathy with the things for which his fellows prayed in their temples: while they petitioned aloud for a sound mind, a fair name, and trustworthiness, their real prayers were for the death of a kinsman or the finding of a treasure. Such people, in order to make their prayers acceptable, would plunge their heads two or three times in the holy waters of the Tiber. [50] Sejanus, the commander of the praetorian cohort under Tiberius, prays [51] for honors and for wealth; but in these he finds, as it were, just so many stories of a lofty tower from which he is doomed to plunge all the farther to his destruction. The Lares to whom Tibullus prays with tenderness and affection, Juvenal represents the Romans of his day invoking as follows: [52] "... Little Lares of mine, whom I usually entreat with flakes of incense or spelt or slender garland, when shall I bag some game to give me security for my declining years, to protect me against the mat and the staff of the mendicant?" The objects of this man's prayer include twenty thousand sesterces in interest, small dishes of plain silver, two sturdy slaves, a "stooping engraver" (curvus caelator), and a painter. These he considers a wretched return for his piety.

No God Involved

We come at this juncture to the one element in a prayer which distinguishes it from an incantation. In a prayer the worshiper addresses a divinity, all-powerful in his sphere, whose will must be won by sacrifice and prayer. In magic, on the other hand, no god is involved. [53]

Of course we must recognize that a prayer, in which a god is addressed, may possess one or all of the characteristics of an incantation; and the more of these elements it contains the closer it will be to pure incantation. There will also be corresponding changes in the psychology of the worshiper; for in the stage between the pure incantation, where no god is involved, and the prayer, in which a god is invoked, there must be times when the worshiper is uncertain whether he himself controls the result or whether there is a controlling force superior to him.

It will be necessary to show how the idea of god, all-powerful in his particular field, developed. In the age of magic, man believes that there is a mysterious quality (mana) residing in things and that this quality, if good (positive mana), can be made useful to him by the performance of a magic act of compulsion, accompanied by an incantation or charm; or, if it be harmful (negative mana), it must be avoided; that, when this is impossible, rites of purification must be performed to rid one of the contagion of the tabooed thing. Gradually, with the failure of magic to do what was expected of it, another stage developed in which spirits, not unlike man himself, with human emotions much like his own—spirits not yet developed into gods in the usual sense of that word—were thought to invest the things about him; and they had to be induced to serve him in much the same way as he would induce his friends to assist him, by entreaty and by offering gifts. There was a term for these undeveloped gods, numina; and the Romans never got far beyond this stage in their conception of gods.

We have tried to show in this chapter that the Roman prayers which have come down to us have certain elements in common with the incantation: they were chanted; they were usually in the form of a command, often uttered in an undervoice; they were, either in whole or in part, repeated; the wording had to be exact; the purpose of many of them was evil. We have, further, tried to show that there was one definite advance in prayer over the incantation, which was the result of a change in the mental attitude of the worshiper; that whereas no divinity was invoked in the incantation, in the prayer a numen or a fully developed god was invoked. Finally, in magic, the volitional element appears in the person; in religion, it rests with the divinity.

CHAPTER VII
Naturalism and Animism

THE SUBJECT of animism was discussed in the introductory chapter, [1] and the reader is referred to the principles laid down there. It remains, however, to enlarge upon and illustrate these principles with special reference to Roman life. But first let us say something about a period which, according to some scholars—who are probably right—antedated animism. To this period the name naturism or naturalism has been given. [2] Man, in this period, conceives of things as living, not because they possess spirits like himself, but because they possess powers, usually evil, such as he observes in lightning, in the wild beast, in the river. Certain it is that the Romans often directly addressed objects, in an entirely impersonal way. We have already noted this in the case of the worshiper at the Festival of Pales, who prays to "the springs and the spirits of the springs." [3] Vesta, too, the Roman goddess of fire, must have been thus addressed; for in her temple there was no cult statue, only the sacred fire—Vesta herself.

In this chapter, then, it will be our purpose to discuss in some detail several elements of nature worship among the Romans: stones and trees; springs, rivers, the sea, rain; fire, both in its helpful and in its harmful aspect. Generally, in the fully developed religions, these objects are worshiped as spirits, if not as gods; but, as we shall see, there is abundant evidence that the objects themselves were also worshiped.

The Worship of Stones

The belief in the sanctity of stones was not uncommon in antiquity. Jacob, we recall, on a certain occasion, used stones for a pillow and on awakening, since he realized, because the Lord had appeared to him in a dream, that the place was sacred, "took the stone that he had put for his pillows, and set it up for a pillar, and poured oil upon the top of it." [4] The pouring of oil upon the stone indicates that Jacob believed that God was in it. Again, when Joshua gave his last charge to the people before his death, he used a stone as witness to his words. We read [5] that he "took a great stone, and set it up there under an oak, that was by the sanctuary of the Lord. And Joshua said unto all the people, Behold, this stone shall be a witness unto us; for it hath heard all the words of the Lord which he spake unto us: it shall be therefore a witness unto you, lest ye deny your God." The Greeks, as we know, worshiped meteoric stones. [6] Thus Zeus was worshiped near Gythion as a stone, probably a meteorite. [7] At Delphi was to be seen the stone which Cronus, as the story had it, swallowed in place of Zeus. [8] Again, in the province of Cyrenaica there was a rock, sacred to the South Wind, which no human hand was permitted to touch. [9] And the image of the Great Mother, brought to Rome in 204 B.C., was simply a rough black meteoric stone. [10]

Survivals of stone worship are to be found among modern Christian peoples. Thus in Galicia, where in pre-Christian times stones were especially worshiped, ardent Catholics of to-day are in the habit of kissing stones in order to add potency to their prayers in the church. [11]

To return to Roman times: Pliny the Elder records [12] an odd superstition about the magic potency of certain stones. It seems that childbirth was eased if a stone, which had, by separate blows, killed a man, a boar, and a bear, was cast over the roof of the house in which a pregnant woman lay.

The magic power of a stone, in all probability a meteorite, to cause rain, we have already noted in the discussion of the aquaelicium. [13] The Aos, in our day, worship sacred stones with sacrifice and prayer and believe that certain boulders control the weather. [14]

In the earliest worship of Jupiter, as Feretrius, on the Capitoline Hill, before the god had a temple or even an altar, the oak was his dwelling place. It was at this oak, as the Romans believed, that Romulus hung the spoils which he had taken from the King of the Caeninenses. [15] In historical times, however, a flint stone, possibly an ax or a knife—a reminiscence of the stone age—was the only representation of the god in the temple. We have noted above, in the passage quoted from Joshua, the close connection between the oak and stones. This is probably due to the fact that both are hard and enduring, a quality which they can communicate magically. Both, too, in ancient Latium, were used to mark the boundaries between farms.

A flint stone in the temple of Jupiter on the Capitol was used by the fetials in making oaths "by Jupiter the Stone." In taking such oaths in private life, the Pater Patratus held the stone in his hand and said: [16] "If I wittingly deceive, then may Jupiter cast me out from my property, leaving the city and the citadel safe, as I now cast away this stone." Again, in making a treaty, a fetial struck the sacrificial pig, first saying: [17] "If (the Roman people) shall be the first to defect (from the terms of this treaty) ... do you then, O Jupiter, so strike the Roman people as I shall here to-day strike this pig ..."

Originally an image of Jupiter was taken along with the fetials into foreign countries, but because of the distances over which it had to be carried as Roman sway was extended, the image was later left at home, and the sacred staff belonging to it was used in its place. [18] This shows once more the primitive manner of thought which makes something which has been in contact with the god serve as the god himself.

The boundaries between farms in ancient Latium were marked by terminal stones or by stocks of trees. Certain of these were regarded as gods and were worshiped from time immemorial. [19] Here we have one of the most primitive types of worship among the Romans. At first, doubtless, the stone itself—a fetish [20]—was worshiped, then the spirit resident in the stone. Terminus seems never to have developed beyond the latter stage. Terminal stones were inserted in place with solemn ceremony. A hole was dug for the stone. Into it the blood of the sacrificial animal was allowed to drip, and into it were thrown the bones and ashes, together with incense and products of the farm. Upon these was rammed the terminal stone, properly oiled and garlanded. In later times, other objects were discovered under the stones—charcoal, shattered earthenware vessels, broken glass, bronze coins, and gypsum.

On February twenty-third, in the country, the Terminalia marked the yearly dramatization of the original ceremony. [21] The owners of adjacent farms adorned their respective sides of the boundary stone with garlands; an altar was erected and fire was brought from the home hearth by the wife. An old man, having chopped up wood and piled it high, started the fire. Into it some of the produce of the farm was thrown three times from a basket. The onlookers made libations of wine. In historical times, the blood of a lamb and a suckling pig and, sometimes, of a kid was sprinkled on the stone; but it seems that in olden times blood sacrifice was forbidden. [22] Feasting and songs in praise of Terminus concluded the rites. The offerings to the stone increased its magic power of warding off evils from the farm and gave it strength to oppose all attempts to change the limits of the farm.

In the city, in the temple of Jupiter on the Capitoline, there was a stone said to be Terminus, and above it was an opening to the sky, for Terminus had to be worshiped in the open air. According to the story, when the foundations were being laid for the temple in the reign of Tarquin the Proud, all the gods save Terminus and Youth could be "moved" from their places by the religious exauguratio.

Trees and Groves

That early peoples looked with awe upon trees, groves, and forests scarcely needs illustration when we recall that in primitive times forests covered vast portions of the earth's surface which are now cultivated fields. Such primeval forests existed in Italy. The house of King Latinus, writes Vergil, [23] was located "in a forest, awful, and hallowed by his ancestors." Classical writers refer to forests which had become mere names in their own day. The Ciminian Forest in

Etruria, for example, was as impregnable and fearful as those of Germany, and even traders refused to pass through it. Once, in a combat between the Etruscans and the Romans, the former fled out in rout into the forest. Scarcely any Roman but the general himself was willing to pursue them. Later, however, when the general's brother volunteered to pass through, attended only by a slave, and succeeded in his attempt—a fact which causes the historian to marvel—the general and his army braved the forest and debouched upon the Etruscan plain beyond. [24]

This feeling of awe in the presence of trees is natural enough to early man. The movement of the tree, with the creaking of its branches and the whispering of its leaves when fanned by the breeze, was sufficient to endow it with personal life. Hence there is frequent mention in Roman literature of "voices" coming from sacred groves. For instance, among the prodigies which preceded a pestilence in the reign of King Tullius was "a loud voice, heard coming from a grove on the mountain top." [25] Again, among the prodigies foreboding the murder of Julius Caesar was "a mighty voice, clearly heard everywhere throughout the silent groves." [26] It was quite natural, then, for the poet Ovid to say, in describing a dark grove of oaks, "a spirit resides here," [27] and for Pliny the Elder to write: [28] "Trees were temples of spirits; and, in accordance with the ancient ritual, the simple country folk even now dedicate to a god a tree which excels its neighbors. For we do not honor statues which glisten with gold and ivory more than our groves and the quietude that reigns in them. . . ." Tibullus, when his duties called him into the fields, would pause in worship at a garlanded tree trunk or an ancient boundary stone. [29] Once after the Emperor Verus had recovered from an illness, Cornelius Fronto, the tutor of Marcus Aurelius, prayed in thanksgiving at every sacred grove and tree. [30]

When a Roman made a clearing in the forest for the pasturing of cattle or the reclamation of new arable land, it was necessary to appease the unknown spirits whose domain had been poached upon, that they might work no ill on the cattle to be pastured or on the crops to be planted there. Cato has left us an account of such a ceremony. [31] As we shall see, it was not only intended as an atoning sacrifice, but also (as in the other sacrifices described by Cato) was thought to add strength to the spirits addressed. We translate such portions of this passage as are necessary for the understanding of the rite:

"A grove should be cleared in the Roman manner as follows. Do so with a pig as an atoning sacrifice, and thus formulate your words: 'If thou art a god, or if thou art a goddess, to whom this spot is sacred, as it is right to make atonement to thee with the sacrifice of a pig ... whether I or some one at my bidding shall do it ... I utter prayers of goodness, that thou mayest be favorable and propitious to me, my home, and my slaves, and my children. To this end, from the offering of the atoning sacrifice of the pig, receive thou strength.' If you are minded to do any digging, offer a second atoning sacrifice in the same way, and say this besides: 'for the sake of doing this work.'"

All peoples have considered groves sacred. We are indebted to Frazer for the following instance: [32] "... not far from Idua Oronn, in Southern Nigeria, there is a sacred grove of Abang 'Ndak, where no branch may be cut nor leaf plucked under pain of death."

According to Apuleius, [33] wayfarers who were religiously inclined would pause at sacred groves, offering apples and uttering prayers. Italy in ancient times was dotted with almost countless sacred groves. In Rome, too, many cults sought the shelter of groves. Perhaps the most famous of these was that of the Arval Brothers. We have already had occasion to mention this grove in connection with the subject of taboo. [34] Originally, iron graving instruments were forbidden in it, but with time the Brothers came to offer an atoning sacrifice before taking the iron instrument into the grove and again after removing it. Curiously enough, several of these inscriptions have survived. [35] From them we learn that two ewe lambs were offered to the Mother of the Lares and two wethers to the Lares themselves.

Another sacred grove which seems to have been thronged with worshipers on February first was that of Helernus, to whom the pontiffs offered a black ox. [36] Hence Helernus must have been a chthonic divinity.

Space will not allow descriptions of the many other sacred groves, of Diana at Aricia, Egeria outside the Porta Capena, Juno at Falerii, and a host of others. The fact that they were so numerous indicates that the ancients held them as especially holy.

Men came to have a feeling of friendly awe for trees and often identified the duration of their own lives with the lives of particular trees. For example, when a palm-shoot grew up between the slabs of stone in front of his house, the Emperor Augustus caused the tree to be transplanted to the inner court, where it shared an honored place with his home gods. [37] Doubtless Augustus believed that there was some connection between the palm tree's life and his own. This belief is world-wide. [38] Again, the Caesars had a grove of laurels at Veli, from which any member of the family who was about to celebrate a triumph took a branch. He afterwards planted a branch in the grove again—probably the same one which he had carried in his triumph. A sympathetic connection was believed to exist between the life of the Caesar who planted the shoot and the life of the laurel itself, for the withering of the tree was prophetic of the death of the Caesar. [39] On the country estate of the Flavians stood an ancient oak which sent forth a branch on each of three occasions when the Empress Vespasia gave birth to a child. [40]

This idea is a primitive survival. Among the savages to-day the belief is persistent that man has an "external soul" [41] which may reside in any object, often a plant of a tree. Thus Frazer informs us [42] that, "Among the M'Bengas in Western Africa, about the Gaboon, when two children are born on the same day, the people plant two trees of the same kind and dance round them. The life of each of the children is believed to be bound up with the life of one of the trees: and if the tree dies or is thrown down, they are sure that the child will soon die ..."

In primitive times, when forests were to be found everywhere, dangerous enemies came from them. What, then, was more natural than for the Romans to perform rites of aversion on the spot where the enemies had appeared? In this way the Romans explained a festival called the Lucaria, which was celebrated in a large wood located between the Salarian Road and the Tiber. According to Festus [43] the reason for the worship of this grove was that the Romans, on one occasion, having been defeated in battle by the Gauls, fled in rout to it for safety. This explanation as given by Festus may contain the truth. However, to understand the Lucaria we need go no further than the universality of the belief in the sanctity of trees, and the reasons which we have already suggested for that belief.

In Rome there were several trees which all Romans held sacred. The Ruminal fig tree on the Palatine Hill—under which, according to the story invented by a later generation to explain the tree, Remus and Romulus had been suckled—was worshiped (originally by shepherds on behalf of their flocks), with offerings of milk. In 58 A.D. the tree, which had been transplanted to the Forum by magic, began to wither, a fact which caused great consternation among the Romans. This consternation disappeared only when the tree began to show signs of reviving. [44] The tree doubtless was worshiped at first; but because the Romans believed that Ruminalis was connected with ruma or rumis, "a teat," they created two new divinities, Jupiter Ruminalis and Rumina. In historical times Rumina had a shrine near the Ruminal fig tree.

On the seventh of July—the Nones of the Goat—the day on which Romulus was believed to have been caught up to heaven at the Swamp of the Goat in the Plain of Mars, women, both bond and free, sacrificed the milky juice of the fig to Juno of the Goat and feasted beneath the sacred wild fig tree. Originally here the tree itself was worshiped. [45]

In the grove at Nemi grew a sacred tree whose boughs only a runaway slave might break. The possession of the branch, popularly identified with the "golden bough" of Vergil, entitled the slave to fight to the death the priest of Diana, the King of the Grove (Rex Nemorensis). If the slave succeeded in killing the priest, he himself became King. It is recorded that Caligula suborned a powerful slave to kill the priest at Nemi who had occupied the office too long to suit the mad emperor. [46]

On the Esquiline Hill was a grove known as the Fagutal, containing a shrine of Jupiter with a beech tree sacred to him. [47]

In Italy all oak trees were sacred to Jupiter. The oldest cult of Jupiter was associated with an oak tree on the Capitoline Hill. Under the cult name Feretrius, Jupiter was, in early times, worshiped as an oak sacred to the shepherds of the community. It was at this tree that Romulus, as the story went, dedicated the arms taken in single combat with the king of the Caeninenses. Later, men peopled the oak with a spirit and built an altar under its shadow. In historical times Jupiter Feretrius was worshiped on this spot in a small temple. With him were associated the fetials whose duties were concerned with treaties and with the declaration of war. [48] Livy records [49] an illuminating instance of the oak conceived of as a spirit. In 458 B.C., the Aequians broke a treaty with the Romans, and, when the Romans sent deputies to the enemy to protest, the Aequian general bade them "tell to the oak" the instructions which they had received from the Roman Senate. One of the deputies on departing said: "Let this consecrated oak and whatever gods exist hear that this treaty has been broken by you." The tree is here felt to have the power to hear the grievances of the Romans against the Aequians.

There was an ancient grove of Juno Lucina on one of the spurs of the Esquiline Hill in which grew an ancient lotus tree called the "hairy" tree (capillata). The reason for this strange name was that the Vestals, when they cut off their hair, suspended it on this tree. Frazer, supporting his conclusion by parallels from Morocco and Germany, believes that the purpose was to prevent the hair from falling into the hands of witches who might work evil upon the good Vestals. [50]

The Romans considered some trees lucky, others unlucky. According to the pontiffs, those trees which bore light-colored fruit were lucky, those which bore dark fruit were unlucky. The same tree—the fig for example—might be lucky or unlucky, depending on whether its figs were light or dark. It is probable, too, that trees which bore no fruit were also thought to be unlucky. [51]

Water

In seeking to understand the worship of water by the Romans, it must be remembered that primitive man associates motion of any sort, whether it be that of swaying branch or dashing cataract or purling stream, with animate life—with spirits. Again, springs bubble from the earth—the seat of mysterious chthonic forces—the same earth which belches forth hot sulphur or mephitic vapors and volcanic lava and ashes. Water, too, possesses healing and cleansing virtues, real and magical. And, finally, the hyperactive imagination of the savage easily led him to believe that the babbling of the springs and rivulets was the voice of the spirits themselves. In the case of the Romans, their dependence upon springs for a supply of cool water during the burning heat of summer tended to add to the sanctity of these springs. Whatever the cause, the Romans, as well, indeed, as all other peoples, considered springs sacred. [52] For example, among the Arabs of Palestine to-day each village has its sacred fountain with special curative powers. [53] Once more, the efficacy of the waters of Lourdes is familiar to every traveler in France. And in England, Protestant as well as Catholic farmers believe that the waters and the moss from the well of St. Walstan, near Norwich, can cure diseases of animals. [54]

The Romans, we find, worshiped springs, not usually, indeed, as gods with statues and all the paraphernalia of a State cult, but as spirits (numina). At the shepherd festival of Pales (we repeat), the farmer calls upon the divinity "to appease the springs and the spirits of the springs." [55] Here, the springs themselves, as distinct from the spirits dwelling in them, are worshiped—a most primitive type of ceremony. Seneca the Philosopher writes as follows about the worship of springs by his fellow countrymen: [56] "We worship the headwaters of great streams; the spot where the giant river breaks forth suddenly from its hidden source has its altars. Hot springs are worshiped by us; and the darkness or unfathomable depth of certain pools renders them sacred."

Once during an illness the epigrammatist Martial was forbidden to drink cooled water; but he disobeyed the prohibition and drank water from a spring in the house of a friend. In spite of this he recovered his health and offered to the spring a sow which he had vowed. [57] Sacred springs, on the other hand, might harm the person who desecrated them. It seems that the Emperor Nero on one occasion took a bath in the sacred source of the Marcian Waters which, according to the tradition, had been brought through aqueducts to

Rome by King Ancus Marcius. An illness which resulted from this imperial caprice was ascribed by the people to the vengeance of the gods for his having polluted the holy waters. [58] The ode of Horace addressed to the spring Bandusia is familiar to all. The poet celebrated the rite, probably on October thirteenth, the day of the Festival of Fons, with sacrifice of a kid and wine and blossoms to the spirit of the spring. [59] On this day chaplets were thrown into springs, and wells were garlanded. [60] Ovid represents Numa, the traditional founder of the Roman religion, sacrificing sheep and offering wine to a spring in a grove at the base of the Aventine Hill. [61]

While we read about a god Fons, and while there was a shrine dedicated to Fons outside Rome near one of its gates, and an altar of Fons on the Janiculum Hill, it is difficult to say with conviction that there was a cult of Fons worshiped under State supervision at a particular temple with priests and sacrifices. It would seem, rather, that the god of fountains was still in a multiple state, like fauns, nymphs and the like, thus representing a transition stage between spirit and god. The presence of so many springs in different parts of Italy, on each of which the people of a particular locality had to depend for their supply of water, would tend to preserve the multiple nature of the god.

We have record of a number of famous springs in Italy. That of Egeria [62] in the sacred grove not far from the Capene Gate on the Appian Road is particularly famous, because from it, in early times at least, the Vestals drew water to cleanse their sacred vessels. This spring still bubbles forth near the Villa Fonseca. [63] According to the story, the worship of Egeria came from the sacred grove of Diana at

Nemi, where the spring poured its healing waters into the lake. Egeria and her sisters the Camenae were worshiped especially by prospective mothers. When the Albans migrated to Rome, they brought the cult with them to the grove of the Muses which, in Juvenal's time, had become a squatting place for indigent Jews; and so the spring itself had lost most of its pristine sanctity.

There was a health-giving spring in Latium near the Numicus River, called Juturna, [64] which Varro placed among "the proper gods and nymphs." The worship of Juturna was transferred to Rome, to the pool near the temple of Vesta in the Forum. It seems likely that in later times the Vestals drew water from this spring rather than from that of Egeria. At any rate its waters were used for sacrificial purposes; and persons who made use of water in their daily occupations celebrated a festival of Juturna in January.

Near the city of Padua, at a place called Aponus in ancient times, were many fissures in the earth, through which burst the crackling flames of sulphur. The water of the near-by lake—called "a present spirit" by Claudian—possessed healing virtues. [65]

The pleasant Roman habit of investing the springs with spirits is illustrated in one of Pliny's letters, where he describes the headwaters of the Clitumnus, a small river in Umbria which flows into a branch of the Tiber. On the banks of the Clitumnus grazed cattle whose brilliant color was due, as the Romans believed, to their having drunk of and bathed in its waters. From the shores of this stream came the white horses which were sacrificed to Jupiter after a triumphal procession to the Capitol. [66] The waters were so clear that Pliny could count, on the bottom, coins which the worshipers had offered to the spirit of the water. [67] Superstition had it that the Clitumnus not only reflected perfectly the human form, but reflected character as well. [68] The spirit of the stream possessed a statue which occupied an ancient temple. That it actually functioned as an oracle in Pliny's day was attested by existing oracular responses attributed to it. Pliny remarks to the friend to whom the letter is addressed that he may perhaps find amusement in reading the countless inscriptions dedicated to the Clitumnus by persons who had been cured by its waters. In the neighborhood, in addition to the temple of Clitumnus, could be found many chapels dedicated to the spirits which presided over the various springs in the neighborhood. Pliny, in another letter, [69] mentions a sacred lake near Ameria, whose waters no ship was allowed to touch. Again, the Elder Pliny notes certain springs at Sinuessa, which were said to have the power to prevent childlessness and to cure insanity, and still others which were especially beneficial in the treatment of sore eyes, ears, or feet, and for healing fractures and wounds of all sorts. [70]

At least one Roman spring was potent to wash away the perjuries of the shady merchant. This was that of Mercury which lay near the Capene Gate. Ovid's description of the rites is illuminating: [71]

"There is a spring of Mercury [he writes] in the neighborhood of the Capene Gate. If you are pleased to believe those who have tested it, the spring possesses a spirit. To it comes the merchant with his tunic caught up; and, being ceremonially pure, he draws water to carry home in an urn which has been fumigated. With this water he drenches a laurel spray, and with the drenched laurel he sprinkles all the wares that are presently to have new owners. He also sprinkles his own hair with the dripping laurel and goes through prayers in a voice which is wont to deceive. 'Wash away past perjuries,' he says, 'wash away my faithless words of the past day.'"

The word numen is here used for the spirit animating the spring; and it is important to note that, as often in the case of water spirits, the water itself is addressed. Furthermore, we observe that a Roman might pray to his gods for evil as well as for good.

There is abundant evidence that rivers were worshiped by the Latins. River water and even the reeds growing along the banks were powerful agents in rites of purification. [72] In the old Roman days auspices were taken by magistrates before crossing a river or any water which arose from a sacred source. This was especially the case with the Petronia, a small tributary of the Tiber. Magistrates regularly took the auspices before crossing this stream to attend to business on the other side. The practice, however, had died out before Cicero's time. [73] Occasionally in magic rites the command was given not to cross a running stream, showing the persistence of the belief that streams resented a person's crossing them. [74]

August twenty-seventh marked the Festival of Volturnus. Now Volturnus was the name of a river in Campania, and as one of the calendars definitely states that the sacrifice was "to the river Volturnus" we may conclude that the festival was originally held in honor of this river. We know that there was a festival of Volturnus held every year at Casilinum, a small town in Campania. [75] But the Festival of Volturnus occurred also in Rome, and so scholars have concluded that Volturnus was an old name for the Tiber. [76] But what is to forbid the transference of the rites of a Campanian river god to

Rome, there to be identified with the Tiber? Such transference was natural to the Romans, as we have seen in the case of the springs Jutuma and Egeria.

The Tiber was considered holy from the earliest days of Rome, and was believed to watch over the homes in the city. [77] The antiquity of its worship is attested by the fact that the Tiber appeared in the "litany" of the pontiffs and in the prayers of the augurs. [78] In one of the fragments of Ennius, [79] we read a portion of a prayer formula, presumably uttered by AEneas: "Thee, Father Tiber, with thy holy stream ..." Servius, commenting on Vergil's imitation of the line, states that the words "Help, Tiber, with thy waters" were part of a formal prayer. The story of Horatius Cocles is familiar to all. As he leaped into the Tiber, he called upon the river to protect him. [80] Horace represents a mother praying that her son be cured of a fever. If the boy is relieved, the mother will make him stand naked in the Tiber. [81] We learn from Persius that when a Roman had prayed for evil—such as the death of a kinsman or a ward—he must plunge his head two or three times in the holy waters of the Tiber in order to make his prayers acceptable. [82] A proposal was laid before the Senate in the reign of Tiberius to change the course of the lakes and streams which emptied into the Tiber. The inhabitants opposed the alteration, protesting that their rivers were under the protection of the gods. [83] At Horta—the modern Orte—there was an altar to Tiber, erected, however, not by a native of the town but by a Roman. Inscriptions indicate that the river god was worshiped at Rome, at Ostia, and elsewhere. [84]

Mommsen has conjectured [85] that the Festival of the Portunalia which occurred on August seventeenth was in honor of the Tiber; and he bases his conclusion on the fact that in the late calendar of Philocalus the day is also called Tibernalia. This seems to be evidence enough to identify the two. But, if this be the case, how are we to explain the keys and the gates which are regularly associated with Portunus? The rites of the Argei offer us a possible clue. On March sixteenth and seventeenth, as we have seen, a solemn procession made a circuit of the twenty-seven chapels called Argei located in various parts of the city. Rush puppets, bearing the same name and resembling bound men, were made in the chapels, where they reposed until May fourteenth and fifteenth, when the pontiffs and generals (Praetores) carried them in procession to the Sublician Bridge. Here the Vestals threw them into the river. The puppets may have represented, by substitution a survival of the time when old men had actually been sacrificed and thrown into the Tiber, possibly to pacify the river god for the building of the bridge. May it not be possible that the keys of Portunus were intended to unlock the various shrines in which the puppets had been placed prior to the procession?

The Romans worshiped not only springs and rivers but the waters of the sea as well. Neptune, afterwards identified with the Greek Poseidon, may possibly have been originally a god of fresh water; [86] certainly the little we know about the Roman Neptune does not point to a sea god.

The Romans were not naturally given to navigation. We read frequently in the Roman poets about the impiety of the man who first entrusted his bark upon the ocean. [87] Evidently there was a strong tradition that it was wrong to sail the sea. When, then, a

Roman was compelled to embark upon the ocean, he performed sacrifice to appease the spirits of the waters. For example, Roman generals before departing by sea against the enemy regularly made sacrifice to the Tempests and to the waves of the sea. [88] There was a temple of the Tempests near the Capene Gate, built by the Scipio who was consul in 259 B.C. after his fleet had been saved from shipwreck off the coast of Corsica. The epitaph of Scipio records the event. [89] Readers of Vergil will remember that in order to secure favorable weather and a safe passage from Sicily, after celebrating games in honor of Anchises, AEneas offered sacrifice and libations to the Winds, to Neptune, and to the sea, before sailing against the enemy. [90] The sacrifice was made both to Neptune and to the sea, showing that a distinction was made between the god and the sea. The sacrifice to the sea was a primitive survival.

This account of water worship may fittingly close with some notice of Jupiter as a rainmaker. In this capacity he is mentioned for the first time in literature by Tibullus. [91] This seems strange in view of the common use of the expression Jupiter Pluvius in our own day. From the earliest times, however, the god was associated with rain-making; the non-appearance of the epithet Pluvius in ancient times may be accounted for by the fact that rain-making was a magic or quasi-magic ceremony, and hence no god need originally have been involved at all. The name Jupiter alone is frequently used by Roman writers for rain. Thus Vergil, in his seventh Eclogue (60), represents one of the shepherds saying: "And Jupiter shall descend in joyous rain."

Fire

Fire, like water, is regularly used to remove the harmful effects of contact with persons and things which are, as we say, taboo, and for driving away evils of all sorts, whether spiritual or physical. Thus persons who attended a Roman funeral had to be sprinkled with water and to walk over fire in order to remove the contagion of death—a rite usually called the "fire walk." [92] Early man may have believed that he could thus set up a fiery barrier between himself and the spirits of the dead which were likely to harrow him. This possibility is suggested by similar rites among other peoples where the avowed purpose is apotropaic. Thus Frazer records [93] that "... The Tumbuku of Central Africa, on the shores of Lake Nyasa, resembled the Romans in practising both the barrier by fire and the barrier by water after a funeral; for on returning from a burial all who had taken part in it washed in a river, and after that, on their way home to the village, they were met by a native doctor or wizard, who kindled a great fire on the path, and all the mourners had to pass through the flames..."

At the Roman Festival of Pales, in April, the farmer, his family, and his flocks jumped through three bonfires of bean straw; [94] the object was to burn away evils, seen and unseen, and, in the case of women, to induce fertility by driving out all interfering influences. Ovid discloses the curious psychology of the worshiper when he says, [95] "Consuming fire cleanses all things and refines the impurities from metal; therefore it cleanses sheep and shepherd." Rites similar to this, in which flocks are driven through bonfires, are common among many peoples. The usual purpose is to ward off witches. Sometimes, however, the object is to assist the growth of crops and flocks. Thus we read: [96] "... at the Beltane fires, formerly kindled in the Highlands of Scotland on May Day (only ten days later than the Palilia), the person who drew the black lot (a piece of oatmeal cake blackened with charcoal) had to leap thrice through the flames for the sake of 'rendering the year productive of the sustenance of man and beast...'"

I give one more illustration, taken from Italian religion. Every year, at the Festival of Apollo Soranus, at the base of Mount Soracte, certain priests called Wolves of Soranus walked barefoot over hot ashes without being burned. [97] This miraculous immunity was due, as Varro suggests, [98] to the fact that they had first treated their feet with some medicated preparation. We are not concerned here with the various problems in connection with the rite, but with the so-called "fire walk" which had many parallels among other peoples, ancient and modern; its purpose was doubtless, as in the case of the Roman "fire walk" after funerals, both cathartic and apotropaic. For similar reasons a bride had to touch fire as well as water. [99]

The Romans employed burning sulphur in magic as well as in religious rites. The reason for its use, in addition to its apotropaic powers as fire, is probably that sulphur possesses disinfectant, and medicinal properties, a fact which the Romans themselves recognized. Moreover, sulphur suggested to the Roman mind hot sulphur springs and volcanoes and the fears that these inspired. Again, the Romans believed that thunderbolts received their light from sulphur and that sulphur fumes accompanied a discharge of lightning.

We shall note a few instances of the magic and religious use of sulphur. Tibullus, while a witch droned incantations, purified his sweetheart Delia with burning sulphur, and thus, by performing an assisting magic rite, restored her to health. [100] In the rites of the Festival of Pales, the shepherds burned sulphur, and its fumes purified the sheep. [101] A similar rite has survived down to modern times in Esthonia, where the people on St. George's Day—within a few days of the time of the ancient Festival of Pales—used to purify the cattle with sulphur as a protection against witches. [102]

Not only sulphur but other combustible substances were used as purifying agents. A witch, for example, purified Tibullus from the harmful effects of magic by using blazing pine torches. [103]

One of the most frequent conceptions among savages is that love is fire and, more particularly, that fire represents the male principle and water the female principle. [104] Hence transition is easy to the belief that maidens may be impregnated by fire. Among the Romans, miraculous impregnation by fire accounted for the birth of Servius Tullius, Romulus and Remus, and the King of Praeneste. Servius has told at length the story of the birth of the latter. He writes: [105]

"... There were once two brothers at Praeneste who were called divine. While their sister was sitting by the hearth, a spark, leaping out, pierced through her womb, and by it, as the story goes, she conceived and subsequently bore a child. She cast the boy away at the Temple of Jupiter. Some maidens, however, who were on their way to procure water, found and picked up the child near a fire which was not far away from the spring. From this circumstance he was called the son of Vulcan ..."

We have noticed the use of fire as a purifying agent in magic and in religious rites and as the male principle in life. We have now to consider fire as a spirit, or, we should rather say, two spirits, for fire in its helpful aspect—in cooking the food and warming the home—was known as Vesta, while as a destructive force it was called Vulcan.

The Romans looked upon fire as a god. Ovid, for example, in a passage in which he seeks to explain the use of fire at the Festival of Pales, calls fire, as well as water, a god. [106]

The origin of the worship of Vesta—fire in its helpful aspect—goes back to primitive days when it was necessary to keep fire alive for the use of the community. The fire was in the care of the unmarried daughters of the family, who were, in reality, the priestesses of the sacred fire in the home. After the main course of the noon meal, silence was commanded, and a portion of the sacred salt-cake, made by the hands of the daughters of the home, was cast from a platter into the fire as a sacrifice to Vesta. [107] As many of the religious forms of the Roman family had their counterpart in the State religion, so the worship of fire in the home had its counterpart in the Roman State religion. [108] The seat of the worship of Vesta in Rome was the circular "temple" of Vesta, shaped like a primitive hut. Here Vesta—the sacred fire of the State—was tended by six maiden priestesses, who renewed it every year, on March first, from a spark formed by friction. [109] There was no statue of Vesta in the "temple": the fire was the goddess herself. This fact shows the persistence with which Vesta resisted the anthropomorphizing influence in Roman religion.

The development of destructive fire into a god was quite natural. Early man saw that fire not only warmed his body and made his food more palatable, but burned down his hut and brought death and destruction in its wake. Vesta, as we have seen, was fire in its helpful aspect; Vulcan, on the contrary, was destructive fire. There is no reason why Vulcan, as fire, should have been worshiped at the hearth with Vesta, for Vesta was never considered a destructive force, nor was Vulcan ever, in historical times at least, considered beneficent. [110] Vergil, Ennius and Roman writers generally gave the name Vulcan to destructive fire. [111] Ostia was the seat of an ancient and flourishing cult of Vulcan, a fact due, doubtless, to the danger in the hot season to the granaries located on the Tiber. Here Vulcan had a temple, a pontiff, and a praetor, also an aedile for performing the sacrifices. [112] At Rome the temple of Vulcan was appropriately located outside the walls of the city; there by rites and sacrifices the city was protected against fire. [113]

Vulcan was concerned in two Roman rites. In June, Fishermen's Games, so-called, were, celebrated across the Tiber by the City Praetor on behalf of the Tiber fishermen. The fish caught by the fishermen were taken, not to market, but to the Square of Vulcan, where they were offered alive on an altar to that god in place of human souls. [114] On August twenty-third occurred the Festival of Vulcan, at a time when his aid would be necessary to avert fires which were likely to break out. Varro informs us [115] that people cast animals (presumably fish) into the fire "in place of themselves." In both these rites, the fish were offered as substitutes for human lives, which were thus to be saved miraculously from destructive fire. The fish, having come from the Tiber whose waters were used to extinguish fires, would be magically effective in preventing them. We gather one additional fact about the festival from one of Pliny's letters, [116] in which we read that, on the night of the Festival of Vulcan, Pliny's uncle used to begin studying at night by lamplight—not, however, Pliny assures us, for luck. It would seem from this statement that the Romans used to light their lamps ceremonially on this night for good luck.

To summarize: We have seen in this chapter that in the period when early man was employing a magic act and an incantation, mechanically, to effect a desired result, he would address various objects in nature directly—a tree, a stone, a spring, a river, the sea, rain—with no feeling that these objects possessed spirits like himself. They were believed to have strange powers, potent for ill. Then, for various reasons which we shall mention shortly, he began to consider that these things possessed spirits much like his own. For he saw that things in nature moved just as he moved; that trees whispered when fanned by the winds; that forests roared when lashed by storms; that springs and rivulets babbled as they flowed; and thus gradually he came to people these objects with spirits like himself. Furthermore, dreams aided him in this; for he found that when he dreamed, his soul would fly away from the body for the time being, and that he would take with him and use the things which he normally had about him in his waking moments. Hence these, too, he peopled with spirits.

We have seen that the belief in the sanctity of stones is common to all peoples, and that the oak and the stone often are closely connected in worship, possibly because of their hard and enduring nature which can be magically communicated to person, thing, or action. Many of the stones worshiped by ancient peoples were meteorites. Thus the Romans used a meteorite in performing magic rites to produce rain. Inasmuch as the stone had fallen from the sky, it was magically equivalent to the sky, and hence could cause it to overflow with rain. A flint stone was the only representation of Jupiter Feretrius in historical times, and before that the oak seems to have been the dwelling place of the god. The flint and the oak were at first worshiped directly. The Romans used this stone in taking oaths and in treatymaking. They furthermore marked off boundaries with stocks and stones, and these were often considered sacred. At first the stone itself was worshiped, and then the spirit resident in it; but we have seen that the worship of the terminal stone probably never developed much further than the fetish stage.

The fact that sparks are produced by striking one stone against another must have created a feeling of awe among primitive peoples. [117]

The Romans, in common with all peoples, considered forests sacred. There were several reasons for this. In the first place, from the forest came dangers of all sorts, particularly wild beasts and enemies. It was natural, then, for early man to perform magic rites of aversion in the place from which these evils had come. Furthermore, trees move; and it is a common observation, as we have already noted, that primitive people associate motion of any sort in nature with animate life. The sounds, too, which came from the forest were, to the imagination of early man, human voices. He thus associated human life with trees, and often identified his own life with that of a particular tree. The death of the tree foreboded his own death. The fact that lightning so often strikes trees and kills persons under them doubtless led early man to fear them.

We are not surprised, then, to find that before a clearing was made in a forest in historical times the numerous spirits of the trees, as well as the evil spirits which haunted the forest, had to be appeased with sacrifice.

We have remarked, further, that the Romans considered water sacred, whether as spring, river, sea, or rain. The reason for this, as in the case of trees, may be partly the fact that primitive man associates motion of any sort with animate life. Further, the resemblance of the purling of springs to the human voice may have aided the animizing process.

The Romans used water from springs and from running streams to wash away the evil effeas of contact with persons and things possessing a mysterious power to harm. Since, in daily life, they found that water cleansed their bodies and their utensils, they believed that it was effective as well in washing away evils, seen and unseen. ne sprinkling of water at religious and magic ceremonies was a survival of an earlier washing. Springs, too, might cause as well as cure disease, if their waters were desecrated. Again, Roman business men had no scruples against using the waters of a holy spring to cleanse themselves and their wares after a shady business transaction.

It was religiously dangerous for a person to cross a running stream and, in certain cases, religious rites had to be performed before doing so. The sanctity of rivers may be due to the fact that every year they took their toll of human life; and this association of the river with the power to harm may ultimately have led to river-worship. Here, again, the motion of the river and the sound of its flowing waters aided the animizing process.

The worship of the sea was of late origin; and this is strange, for the Romans early came to dread that restless expanse which so often destroyed human life, which threw up on its shores strange creatures, and which later brought dangerous enemies; further, the curious rise and fall of its surface and the mysterious rhythmic churning of its waters added to its uncanniness. And so the Romans avoided the sea.

One of the earliest Roman worships was that of rain. Here, again, rain itself was addressed first, and then Jupiter, the maker of rain. Rain and Jupiter are often synonymous. Rain has the power to harm. It must, therefore, be induced to do good. Furthermore, the fact that rain came from the sky and was associated with destructive lightnings added an element of religious awe to it.

We have seen that the Romans regularly employed fire in magic and in religious rites in order to remove the harmful effects of contact with objects possessing dangerous powers—corpses, for instance. Furthermore, like savages of to-day, they set up bonfires and the "fire walk" as barriers between themselves and the spirits of the dead. This use of fire was both cathartic (to remove evils actually present) and apotropaic (to keep away potential evils, such as the spirits of the dead).

In rites of purification, sulphur was commonly used, because of the purificatory powers possessed by the fire itself. Further, sulphur possesses medicinal and disinfectant properties. Coupled with this, in the mind of the worshiper, were the association with awesome sulphur springs and volcanoes and the belief that lightning received its light from sulphur.

The Romans, in common with savages of to-day, believed that fire was the male principle in life. Consistently with this belief, they explained certain miraculous births through impregnation of a virgin by a spark from the hearth.

Fire in its helpful aspect was called Vesta; fire as a destructive force was known as Vulcan. Vesta never outgrew her character as a mere spirit, for the sacred fire was her only representation in the "temple" of Vesta. The conception of a god of destructive fire grew quite naturally from the realization that fire not only helped but also harmed.

Doubtless, at first, fire was conceived of as a single spirit. Hence it was possible for men to think of a maiden as impregnated by a spark from a hearth, whose fire, in historical times, was conceived of as feminine. With the growth in knowledge of the uses of fire in cooking and heating, this phase of fire became feminine, because fire for such purposes was employed by women in the house. The fire, however, which destroyed the forest had all the force of man, and so was considered masculine.

CHAPTER I FOOTNOTES:

1 Aulus Gellius, Noctes Atticae IX, 13:6-19 (quoting Quintus Claudius Quadrigarius). The story, to be sure, may have been invented to explain why the family had the necklace as an emblem, but for our purpose this matters little. The Romans believed it to be a possible explanation, and that is enough to assist us in understanding the psychology underlying such stories.

2 Suetonius, Caligula XXXV, 1.

3 Acta SS. Perpetuae et Felicitatis Martyrum, 57 (in Migne, Vol. III, p. 57).

4 Quoted from the Chicago Tribune in George W. Gilmore, Animism, p. 15.

5 Noctes Atticae XX. 10, 8-9.

6 Metamorphoses II. 21-26.

7 Charles G. Leland, The Unpublished Legends of Vergil, pp. 45-49.

8 Tusculanae Disputationes I. 36.

9 De Rerum Natura V. 925-926.

10 Fasti I. 185-188.

11 Apologia XXXIV.

12 Servius on Vergil's Aeneid II. 116.

13 W. Warde Fowler, The Religious Experience of the Roman People, p. 3.

14 De Rerum Natura V. 953-957. 982-998, 1007-1008.

15 De Divinatione II. 18, 42.

16 See R. R. Marett, On the Threshold of Religion, P. 137.

17 Marett, in a private letter to W. Warde Fowler (quoted in the latter's The Religious Experience of the Roman People, p. 42, note 4) writes as follows: "In taboo the mystic thing is not to be lightly approached (negative aspect); qua mana, it is instinct with mystic power (positive aspect)."

18 See Edward Clodd, Animism; George W. Gilmore, Animism; F. B. jevons, The Idea of God, pp. 15-18.

19 Apuleius, Metamorphoses VI. 12.

20 E. B. Tylor, Primitive Culture, Vol. 1, Chapter XI.

21 J. G. Frazer, Taboo, pp. 36-37.

22 Carveth Wells, Six Years in The Malay Jungle, pp. 73-74.

23 De Rerum Natura IV. 453-461.

24 Naturalis Historia VII. 52, 174.

25 Ibid. II. 7, 16; Petronius, Satyricon XVII.

26 Metamorphoses I. 13.

27 Fasti IV. 759-760.

28 I have already treated this subject in an article entitled "The Magic Elements in Roman Prayers," in Classical Philology, XXV (1930). pp. 47-55.

CHAPTER II FOOTNOTES

1   Chapter IV, pp. 124-126.
2   Aelius Lampridius, Commodus Anioninus XVI. 6.
3   The Religious Experience of the Roman People, P. 33.
4   Primitive Culture in Italy, pp. 193-194.
5   Naturales Quaestiones IV(b). 7, 2.
6   See Frazer, The Golden Bough, Vol. II, pp. 253-254.
7   I. 5, 49.
8   Fasti II. 45-46.
9   Servius on Vergil's Aeneid V. 79.
10 Genesis IX. 4; Leviticus XVII. 11-14.
11 Livy XXIV. 10; Plutarch, Romulus XXIV; Vergil, Georgica I. 485; Apuleius, Metamorphoses IX. 34; Cicero, De Divinatione I. 98.
12 Livy III. 10. 6.
13 Livy XXII. 36.
14 Livy XXII. 1.
15 Livy I. 48, 7.
16 Livy XXI. 63.
17 Livy III. 18, 10.
18 Suetonius, Caligula LVII. 4.
19 Suetonius, Domilian IX. 1.
20 Sallust, Bellum Catilinum XXII. 1-2.
21 Tacitus, Annales I. 44.
22 Livy I. 59, 1.
23 Noctes Atticae X. 8.
24 See Ovid, Fasti I. 349-350; Vergil, Georgica II. 536-537; Plutarch, Numa XII. 1.
25 Ovid, Fasti I. 349.
26 Varro in Censorinus III.
27 Ovid, Fasti III. 811.
28 Tacitus, Historiae II. 3; Plutarch, Quaestiones Romanae XV.
29 Romulus XII. 1; Solinus I. 19.
30 The Religious Experience of the Roman People, p. 33.
31 Aulus Gellius, Noctes Atticae X. 15, 12; see Frazer, Taboo, Vol. II, p. 239; Leviticus VII. 26.
32 Quaestiones Romanae CX.
33 Julius Capitolinus, Maximus et Balbinus V. 3-4.
34 Festus: Ederam (Mueller, p. 82) ; Plutarch, Quaestiones Romanae CXII.
35 The Golden Bough, Vol. II. pp. 259-264.
36 See Chapter III, Knots, pp. 109-112.
37 Fasti IV. 657-658.
38 Tacitus, Annales II. 14.
39 Vergil, Aeneid II. 717.
40 Festus: October equus (Mueller. p. 178).
41 Ovid, Fasti IV. 721-862.
42 Plutarch, Romulus XXI; Fowler, The Roman Festivals, p. 311.
43 Siculus Flaccus in Gromatici Veleres I. 141.
44 The Idea of God, p. 5.
45 Livy I. 32, 12.
46 Festus: Laureati (Mueller, p. 117).
47 Servius on Vergil's Aeneid XII. 120; Pliny, Naturalis Historia XXII. 5.
48 Festus: Armilustrium (Mueller, p. 19); Charisius I (Keil, p. 81); Varro, De Lingua Latina V. 153, VI. 22.
49 Fowler, The Religious Experience of The Roman People, pp. 97 and 217.
50 Livy I. 28, 1.
51 Frazer, The Fasti of Ovid, Vol. II, p. 235.
52 Annales II. 17.
53 Fred Puleston, African Drums, p. 95.
54 Aelius Spartianus, Septimius Severus XI. 8.
55 Leviticus XII. 2-4.
56 Ibid. XII. 2-4.
57 Ibid. XII. 4.
58 Ibid. XV. 19.
59 Naturalis Historia VII. 63.
60 Glimpses of Unfamiliar Japan, p. 126.
61 The Herald Tribune (New York City), February 4, 1930, p. 2.
62 Cato, De Agricultura LXXXIII.
63 Macrobius, Saturnalia I. 12, 28; Propertius V. 9 (Lucian Mueller) ; see Frazer, The Fasti of Ovid, Vol. II, p. 215.

64 The Roman Festivals, p. 143.

65 Tertullian, Ad Nationes II. 7.

66 The Fasti of Ovid, Vol. II. p. 217.

67 Festus: Exesto (Mueller, p. 82).

68 Gellius, Noctes Atticae IV. 3. 3.

69 Cato, De Agricultura CXLIII. 2.

70 Ovid, Fasti II. 645-646.

71 Ovid, Fasti III. 725-726; Varro, De Lingua Latina VI. 14.

72 Horace, Sermones 1. 9.

73 Horace, Epodi V.

74 Satyricon LXIII.

75 Lucan, Bellum Civile VI. 557-558.

76 Aelius Lampridius, Diadumenus Antoninus IV. 2.

77 Pliny, Epistulae VI. 2, 2.

78 In Vatinium XIV.

79 Apologia I. 18.

80 Aelius Lampridius, Heliogabalus VIII. 1-2.

81 Macrobius, Saturnalia I. 7, 34-35.

82 Apuleius, Apologia XLII-XLIII.

83 Gellius, Noctes Atticae I. 12.

84 De Divinatione I. 46, 103.

85 XXIV. 10.

86 Aelius Spartianus, Didius Julianus VII. 10-11.

87 See Eli E. Burriss, in Classical Philology, XXIV (1929), pp. 151-153.

88 T. W. Thompson, Journal of the Gypsy Folklore Society VIII (1929), pp. 33-39.

89 Caesar, Bellum Gallicum VI. 18.

90 De Civitate Dei VI. 9.

91 See W. Warde Fowler, in Classical Review, X (1896), p. 317.

92 See Frazer, The Fasti of Ovid, Vol. III, p. 139.

93 Fasti VI. 155-162.

94 I. 24, 8.

95 II. 31-34.

96 Tertullian, Ad Nationes II. 11; Lactantius, Institutiones I. 20, 36.

97 Naturalis Historia VII. 6.

98 Ibid., VII. 7.

99 Ibid., VII. 15.

100 Ibid., VII. 3.

101 Ibis., VII. 3.

102 Julius Capitolinus, Clodius Albinus V. 9.

103 Suetonius, Vespasianus V. 2.

104 Tertullian, Ad Nationes II. 11.

105 By H. J. Rose in Primitive Culture in Italy, p. 133.

106 Fasti I. 629-633. See E. S. McCartney, Sex Determination and Sex Control in Antiquity, in American Journal of Philology, XLIII, pp. 62-70.

107 The Roman Festivals, p. 292.

108 Fasti I. 629.

109 See Frazer. The Fasti of Ovid, Vol. II, p. 181.

110 Festus: Egeriae nymphae (Mueller, p. 77).

111 Pliny, Naturalis Historia XXXI. 9.

112 Festus: Lustrici (Mueller, p. 120).

113 Ovid, Fasti III. 771-777; Persius V. 30-31; Suetonius, Divus Julius LXXXIV. 4; De Rhetoribus I; Festus: Bulla aurea (Mueller, p. 36) ; Macrobius, Saturnalia I. 6, 16; Plutarch, Romulus XXV. 5, Quaestiones Romanae CI.

114 H. J. Rose, Primitive Culture in Italy, p. 135.

115 Incertus Auctor, De Praenominibus III (text at the end of C. Kempfe's edition of Valerius Maximus).

116 See Frazer, The Fasti of Ovid, Vol. IV, p. 186.

117 Pliny the Elder, Naturalis Historia VII, 72.

118 Epistulae V. 8.

119 Horace, Carmina III. 23, 17; see Fowler, The Religious Experience of the Roman People, p. 74.

120 Servius on Vergil's Aeneid I. 730.

121 Ovid, Fasti II. 650-652.

122 I. 10. 15-16.

123 Servius on Vergil's Aeneid XI. 543; Festus: Camillus (Mueller, p. 43).

124 Festus: Patrimi et matrimi pueri (Mueller, p. 245).

125 See Frazer, The Fasti of Ovid, Vol. II, pp. 200-201.

126 Carmen Saeculare, passim. See E. S. McCartney, "The Role of the Child in Supplications," in The Classical Weekly, XXII, p. 151.

127 Ernest Crawley, Studies of Savages and Sex, p. 178.

128 Lafcadio Hearn, Glimpses of Unfamiliar Japan, p. 125.

129 Numbers V. 2.

130 Numbers XIX. 11-16.

131 Apuleius, Metamorphoses II. 21-26; see also Lucan, Bellum Civile Vi. 529-537.

132 Epodi V.

133 See Theda Kenyon, Witches Still Live, Chapter XXV.

134 Petronius, Satyricon CXXXIV. 1.

135 Satyricon LIV.

136 Velleius Paterculus II. 4, 6.

137 Plutarch, Flaminius VII. 4.

138 Livy II. 8. 6-7.

139 Livy III. 22. 1.

140 Tacitus, Annales I. 62.

141 Gellius, Noctes Atticae XVI. 4. 4.

142 Festus: Aqua et igni (Mueller, p. 2).

143 Fasti II. 23; see Festus: Everriator (Mueller, p. 77).

144 Frazer, The Fasti of Ovid, Vol. II, p. 279.

145 Frazer, The Fasli of Ovid, Vol. II, pp. 279-283.

146 Festus: Patrimi (Mueller, p. 245).

147 Frazer, The Fasti of Ovid, Vol. 11, p. 197.

148 Gellius, Noctes Atticae X. 15.24.

149 Servius on Vergil's Aeneid III. 64.

150 Ovid, Fasti II. 557-564.

151 Cicero, De Legibus II. 23-58.

152 Servius on Vergil's Aeneid XI. 206.

153 Gaius, Institutiones II. 4.

154 Varro, De Lingua Latina V. 157. On sacer as equivalent to taboo see Frazer's article on "Taboo" in the Encyclopedia Britannica, Vol. xxiii.

155 Ovid, Fasti I. 627-629.

156 Varro, De Lingua Latina VII. 84.

157 Festus: Mortuae pecudis (Mueller, p. 161).

158 Leviticus XI. 39; see also Leviticus VII. 24.

159 Ovid, Fasti II. 283-284.

160 Petronius, Satyricon XLIV.

161 See Fasti VI. 397.

162 Ovid, Fasti I. 57-58; Festus: Religiosus (Mueller, p. 278); Varro, De Lingua Latina VI. 29; Livy VI. 1, 11; Macrobius, Saturnalia I. 15, 22, I. 16, 21-25; Gellius, Noctes Atticae V. 17, 1-2; Festus Nonarum (Mueller, p. 178); Plutarch, Quaestiones Romanae XXV.

163 Livy XXII. 10.

164 I owe this explanation to Frazer, The Fasti of Ovid, Vol. II, pp. 79-82.

165 Festus: Mundus and Mundum (Mueller, pp. 154 and 156) Macrobius, Saturnalia 1. 16, 16-18 (quoting Varro).

166 Joannes Lydus, De Mensibus XIV. 29 (Wuensch): see Ovid, Fasti II. 557-558. 563-564.

167 The Religious Experience of the Roman People, p. 40.

168 Festus: Nonarum (Mueller, p. 178).

CHAPTER III FOOTNOTES

1   Columella, De Re Rustica IX. 14, 3.
2   For the Vestals, see Plutarch, Numa X; Gellius, Noctes Atticae I. 12; Frazer's note on Ovid, Fasti VI. 283.
3   Livy I. 11. 6-9.
4   Livy II. 42, 10-11.
5   Livy VIII. 15, 7-8.
6   Livy XXII. 57.
7   Sallust, Bellum Catilinum XV. 1; Orosius VI. 3; Cicero, Oratio in Toga Candida.
8   Suetonius, Nero XXVIII. 1.
9   IV. 8-10; see Mayor's notes on these lines.
10 Suetonius, Domitianus VIII. 3-4; see Pliny, Epistulae IV. 11, 6.
11 IV. 44, 11-12.
12 Plutarch, Numa X.
13 See W. Warde Fowler, The Roman Festivals, p. 94.
14 Apuleius, Apologia LXXXVIII.
15 Ovid, Metamorphoses X. 431-435.
16 Tibullus II. 1. 11-12.
17 See Fowler, The Roman Festivals, pp. 114-115.
18 Servius on Vergil's Bucolica VIII. 82.
19 Fasti VI. 459-460.
20 V. 8, 1-14; see Frazer, The Fasti of Ovid, Vol. II, pp. 296-297.
21 Amaury Talbot, Life in Southern Nigeria, p. 220.
22 Ovid, Fasti VI. 227-232.
23 Ovid, Metamorphoses X. 431-435.
24 Livy XXXIX. 9. 4. XXXIX. 10, 1. XXXIX. 11, 2; Ovid, Fasti II. 327-330.
25 Aelius Lampridius, Severus Alexander XXIX. 2.
26 Columella, De Re Rustica XII. 4, 2ff.
27 Tolemism and Exogamy, Vol. II, p. 411.
28 Frazer, The Fasti of Ovid, Vol. IV. pp. 205-206.
29 III. 31, 1-2; see also III. 26, 15-16 (Lucian Mueller's edition).
30 I. 3. 23-26.
31 Aelius Spartianus, Pescennius Niger VI. 7.
32 Columella, De Re Rustica XII. 4. 2ff.
33 Ovid, Fasti V. 153-156; see also Tibullus III. 5, 7-8.
34 Plutarch, Caesar IX-X; see Dio Cassius XXXVII. 35 and 45.
35 Ovid, Fasti VI. 437-454; Lactantius, Divinae Institutiones III. 20; Aelius Lampridius, Antoninus Heliogabalus VI. 7.
36 Epistulae IV. 11, 9.
37 Plutarch, Quaestiones Romanae III.
38 Tusculanae Disputasiones IV. 11. 27.
39 Servius on Vergil's Aeneid VIII. 269.
40 Pliny, Naturalis Historia VII. 2, 15.
41 Livy I. 40, 2.
42 Livy XXIII. 5.
43 Livy XXVI. 34, 12; see Macrobius, Saturnalia III. 3, 1.
44 Livy II. 37. 9.
45 Gellius, Noctes Atticae VI. 19, 7.
46 Festus: aesto (Mueller, p. 82).
47 Gellius, Noctes Atticae I. 12. 8.
48 The translation is that of H. J. Rose in Primitive Culture in Italy, p. 67.
49 Pliny, Naturalis Historia XXII. 1, 5.
50 Livy I. 24, 4-6.
51 Livy IV. 3, 9, and 2. 5-7.
52 Livy X. 6.
53 Livy I. 34. 11.
54 Westermarck, The Origin and Development of Moral Ideas, I. 570ff., 590ff.
55 Tylor, Primitive Culture, Vol. I, p. 114,
56 Bellum Gallicum VI. 23.
57 See W. Warde Fowler, The Religious Experience of the Roman People, pp. 223-247.
58 See Frazer, The Fasti of Ovid, Vol. IV, pp. 290-291.
59 Livy II. 36. 1.
60 Cicero, De Haruspicum Responso XI-XII.

61 Livy I. 7, 12-14.
62 Gellius, Noctes Atticae I. 12. 5.
63 Ovid, Fasti VI. 481; Plutarch, Quaes-
    tiones Romanae XVI.
64 Cato, De Agricultura V. 1-4; Dionysius of
    Halicarnassus,
65 Antiquitates Romanae IV. 14, 3-4.
66 Ovid, Fasti VI. 783-784. Seneca, De
    Clementia 1. 18, 2.
67 Dionysius of Halicarnassus IV. 14, 3-4.
68 Suetonius, Claudius XXII.
69 Tacitus, Annales XIV. 21.
70 Apuleius, Metamorphoses IV. 11.
71 Tibullus III. 2. 15-22.
72 Livy IV. 20. 7.
73 Suctonius, Galba XIX.1.
74 Propertius V. 3. 64.
75 On Vergil's Aeneid XII. 120.
76 Ibidem.
77 Cornelius Fronto, Ad Marcum Caesarem
    IV. 4.
78 Livy IV. 7. 12.
79 Livy X. 38.
80 Pliny, Naturalis Historia 11. 56, 147.
81 Ovid, Fasti III. 30.
82 Fasti II. 21.
83 Servius on Vergil's Aeneid IV. 137.
84 Livy I. 32. 6.
85 Pilae effigies (Mueller, p. 239) ; Laneae
(p. 121). Macrobius, Saturnalia I. 7, 35.
86 Pliny, Naturalis Historia XXX. 1, 12.
87 Ovid, Fasti IV, 652-660.
88 See Chapter 1, pp. 5-7.
89 Tibullus I. 3. 30.
90 Apologia LVI.
91 Leviticus VI. 10.
92 Leviticus XVI. 4.
93 Tibullus I. 5, 15-17.
94 Vergil, Bucolica VIII.
95 J. G. Frazer, The Fasti of Ovid, Vol. III, p.
    61.
96 IV. 518.
97 Gellius, Noctes Atticae X. 15, 30.

98 Ovid, Fasti VI. 227-232.
99 Ibid., III. 397-398.
100 Ovid, Fasti IV. 854; Plutarch, Quaes-
    tiones Romanae XIV; Tibullus III. 2. 11.
101 Ovid, Fasti III. 257-258.
102 Servius on Vergil's Aeneid IV. 518.
103 Ovid, Metamorphoses IV. 297-300.
104 Apuleius, Metamorphoses III. 1.
105 Vergil, Aeneid IV. 518.
106 Servius on Vergil's Aeneid IV. 518.
107 Gellius, Noctes Atticae X. 15, 9.
108 Plutarch, Quaestiones Romanae CXII;
    Gellius, Noctes Atticae X. 15, 13; Festus,
    Ederam (Mueller, p. 82).
109 Livy I. 18, 7.
110 Ovid, Farii V. 432.
111 Juvenal XII. 3-6.
112 Tibullus II. 1, 7; Ovid, Fasti I. 83, III. 375-
    376, IV. 335-336.
113 Naturalis Historia XXVIII. 28.
114 Tibullus II. 1, 10.
115 Gellius, Noctes Atticae X. 15, 6.
116 Ovid, Fasti IV. 657-658.
117 Servius on Vergil's Aeneid III. 370.
118 See J. G. Frazer, The Golden Bough, Vol.
    II, p. 230.
119 M. Cary and A. D. Nock, in The Classical
    Quarterly, XXI (1927), pp. 125-127; see
    Propertius V. 5, 9-10.
120 Claudius Claudianus, Carminum Mi-
    norum Corpusculum XXIX. 25-27.
121 De Agricultura CLX.
122 See Frank Granger, The Worship of the
    Romans, p. 164.
123 Pliny, Naturalis Historia X. 54, 152.
124 Henzen, Acta Fratrum Artalium, pp.
    128-135.
125 Pliny, Naturalis Historia XXXVI. 15, 100;
    Dio III. 45.
126 Pliny, Naturalis Historia XXXVI. 100.
127 I Kings VI. 7.
128 Dessau, Inscriptiones Latinae Selectae
    4906.

129 On Vergil's Aeneid II. 57; see also Gellius, Noctes Atticae X. 15, 8.

130 W. Warde Fowler, The Religious Experience of the Roman People, p. 32.

131 Aeneid IV. 513; see also Macrobius, Saturnalia V. 19, 7-14; Ovid, Metamorphoses VII. 227.

132 Ovid, Fasti 11. 575-578.

133 I. 85; VIII. 49, 50; see Tavenner, op. cit. p. 121, note 294.

134 Plutarch, Romulus XI. 2; Zollaras VII. 3.

135 Macrobius, Saturnalia V. 19, 13.

136 Servius on Vergil's Aeneid I. 448.

137 Festus: Infibulati (Mueller, p. 113).

138 Livy I. 20, 4.

139 Claudianus, De Bello Gothico 233-234.

140 Annales 1. 28.

141 J. G. Frazer, The Fasti of Ovid, Vol. IV, p. 48.

142 Juvenal XIII. 223-224.

143 Festus: Fulguritum (Mueller, p. 92) ; Bidental (p. 33). Fowler, The Religious Experience of the Roman People, p. 37. Wissowa, Religion und Kultus der Romer, p. 122 and note 3.

144 Festus: Bidental (Mueller, P. 33) ; Horace, Ars Poetica 470-472.

145 See Wissowa, op. cit,, P. 131,

146 Tacitus, Annales XIII. 24.

147 Suetonius, Galba IV. 2.

148 Festus: Occisum (Mueller, p. 178).

149 Pliny, Naturalis Historia II. 145.

150 Ovid, Fasti II. 201-202; Livy II. 49, 8.

151 Translated in Comparetti, Vergil in the Middle Ages, p. 261.

CHAPTER IV FOOTNOTES

1   Andrew Lang, Myth, Ritual and Religion, Vol. 1, pp. 94-95.
2   Noctes Atticae XX. 8; see also Pliny, Naturalis Historia II. 41, 109.
3   Ovid, Fasti VI. 101-106.
4   Macrobius, Saturnalia I. 12. 31-33.
5   The Roman Festivals, p. 131.
6   Fasti VI. 155-162. I have already made use of this excerpt in another connection; but its appropriateness for our present purpose compels me to repeat it here.
7   Livy I. 24, 8.
8   Fasti VI. 129-130.
9   See Frazer, The Fasti of Ovid, Vol. IV, p. 142.
10 Frazer, loc. cit.
11 Ibid., Vol. II, p. 446.
12 Fasti II. 571-582.
13 See Frazer, The Fasti of Ovid, Vol. II, pp. 447-448.
14 Claudius Claudianus, In Rufinum II. 488-490.
15 Numa VIII. 6.
16 Tertullian, Apologeticus adversus Gentes pro Cbristianis V; Julius Capitolinus, Marcus Antoninus XXIV. 4.
17 Dion Cassius LXXI. 8-10.
18 The Magic Art, P. 307.
19 Ancient sources for this rite are: Festus: Aquaelicium (Mueller's edition, p. 2); Ibid.: Manalem lapidem (p. 128); Tertullian, Apologeticus XL; De Ieiunio XVI; Servius on Vergil's Aeneid III. 175; Varro, De Lingua Latina VI. 94; Livy I. 20, 7; Ovid, Fasti III. 327-328; Arnobius V. I; Plutarch, Numa XV; Pliny, Naturalis Historia II. 140, XXVIII. 14.
20 Fasti III. 324-325. Note that Jupiter, i.e., rain, is to be brought down from heaven by sheer magic.
21 Satyricon XLIV.
22 Manalem lapidem (Mueller's edition, p. 128).
23 De Ieiunio XVI.
24 Ancient sources for this rite are: Dionysius of Halicarnassus, Antiquitates Romanae I. 37, 3; Ovid, Fasti III. 791-792, V. 621-622; Varro, De Lingua Latina V. 45-54, VII. 44; Plutarch, Quaestiones Romanae XXXII; Festus: Sexagenarios (Mueller's edition, P. 334). The best summary of the views of modern scholars is contained in Frazer's note to Ovid, Fasti V. 621-622.
25 Loc. cit.
26 Georg Wissowa, Religion und Kultus der Romer, p. 421.
27 The Roman Festivals, pp. 116-121.
28 See H. J. Rose, Primitive Culture in Italy, pp. 103-io4.
29 For this rite see: Varro, Res Rusticae I. 1, 6, De Lingua Latina VI. 16; Ovid, Fasti IV. 901-942; Servius on Vergil's Georgica I. 151; Columella, De Re Rustica X. 342; Tertullian, De Spectaculis XV; Lactantius I. 20, 17; Festus: Catularia (Mueller's edition, p. 45), Robigalia (p. 267) ; Pliny, Naturalis Historia XVIII. 14; C. I. L. I, pp. 231, 316.
30 Fasti IV. 941-942.
31 De Spectaculis V.
32 For this rite see: Festus: Horda (Mueller's edition, p. 102) Varro, Res Rusticae II. 5, 6-7; De Lingua Latina VI. 15; Lydus, De Mensibus IV. 49 and 72; Ovid, Fasti IV. 629-672, 731-740.
33 Fasti IV. 633-634.
34 See Joannes Lydus, De Mensibus IV. 72.
35 Chapter V.
36 Fasti IV. 681-712.
37 Frazer, The Fasti of Ovid, Vol. III, p. 331; see also Rose, Primitive Culture in Italy, pp. 50-51.

CHAPTER V FOOTNOTES

1 Gellius, Noctes Afficae IV. 3, 3.
2 G. Henzen, Acta Fratrum Arvalium, pp. 128-135.
3 Livy II. 36, 1.
4 See Varro, De Lingua Latina VI. 13, 34; Ovid, Fasti II. 1936, and Frazer's notes on these lines. The word februum is of Sabine origin. See Varro. loc. cit.
5 For this festival see especially Tibullus II. 5, 87-106; Propertius V. 4, 73-78; Ovid, Fasti IV. 721-782; see also Frazer's notes on Ovid, Fasti IV. 721-782.
6 Ovid, Fasti IV. 807-820; Plutarch, Romulus XII. 1.
7 Plutarch, loc. cit.; Solinus I. 19.
8 J. G. Frazer, The Fasti of Ovid, Vol. III, P. 339.
9 Livy I. 45, 4-7.
10 Festus: Aqua et igni (Mueller, pp. 2-3).
11 Aeneid II. 717-720.
12 Ovid, Fasti IV. 314-315.
13 Ovid, Fasti IV. 736 and 778.
14 Epodi V. 25-26.
15 Aeneid IV. 512.
16 Fasti VI. 157. See a paper entitled The House Door in Greek and Roman Religion and Folk Lore, by Professor M. B. Ogle, American Journal of Philology XXXII (1911), pp. 251-271.
17 Festus: Aqua et igni (Mueller, pp. 2-3).
18 Claudianus, De Sexto Consulatu Honorii Augusti 324-330.
19 I. 2. 61.
20 Catullus LXI. 15.
21 Fasti II. 27-28.
22 Nemesianus IV. 62.
23 Ovid, Fasti IV. 728.
24 Festus: Laureati (Mueller, p. 117).
25 Servius on Vergil's Aeneid XII. 120.
26 Livy I. 24, 4-9.
27 Everriator (Mueller, p. 77).
28 Fast; II. 2 3-24.
29 The Fasti of Ovid, Vol. II, p. 279.
30 See Thomas J. Marett, in Folk Lore XXXVIII (1927), p. 181; Peter J. Hamilton, in Folk Lore XXXVIII (1927), p. 62.
31 De Civitate Dei VI. 9.
32 See above, pp. 148-150.
33 Festus: Stercus (Mueller, P. 344).
34 Ovid, Fasti VI. 713-714.
35 Frazer, The Fasti of Ovid, Vol. IV, pp. 314-315.
36 W. Warde Fowler, The Religious Experience of the Roman People, P. 136.
37 Plutarch, Numa X.
38 For an excellent account of the Lupercalia see Frazer, The Fasti of Ovid, Vol. II, pp. 327-341, with the references there given.
39 Justin Martyr XLIII. 1, 7.
40 On Vergil's Aeneid II. 116.
41 See Apuleius, Apologia LXXXVIII.
42 For this rite see Varro, De Lingua Latina VI. 18; Plutarch, Romulus XXIX, Camillus XXXIII; Macrobius, Saturnalia I. 11, 36-42; Ausonius, De Feriis, 9-10; Frazer, op, cit., Vol. II, pp. 343-356.
43 Loc. cit.
44 Fragments of Hipponax (in Tzetzes, Hist. XXIII. 726-756); see Servius on Vergil's Aeneid III. 57.
45 L. Preller, Romische Mythologie, I. 287.
46 Pliny, Naturalis Historia XXI. 42, XXV. 50.
47 Eugene Stock McCartney, "Magic Circles as Barriers to Snakes," in The Classical Weekly, Vol. XXII (1929), pp. 175-176.
48 Ovid, Fasti IV. 825-826; Servius on Vergil's Aeneid IV. 212; Festus: Primigenius sulcus (Mueller, p. 237) ; Varro, De Lingua Latina V. 143, Res Ruslicae II. 1, 10; Plutarch, Romulus XI. 1-2, Quaestiones Romanae XXVII; Isidore, Originer XV. 2, 3; Columella, De Re Rustica VI, Praefatio VII; see also Frazer, The Fasti of Ovid, Vol. III, pp. 379-384; Fowler, The Religious Experience of the Roman People, P. 214.

49 See Chapter III, p. 118.
50 Servius on Vergil's Bucolica III. 77.
51 De Agricultura CXLI. 1-3; see E. G. Sihler, Testimonium Animae, pp. 342-344.
52 See W. Warde Fowler. The Roman Festivals, P. 89.
53 W. Warde Fowler. The Religious Experience of the Roman People, pp. 182-183.
54 Ibid., pp. 132-133.
55 For the Salian priests see Festus: Mamuri Veturi (Mueller, P. 131); Dionysius of Halicarnassus, Antiquitates Romanae II. 71; Plutarch, Numa XIII; Servius on Vergil's Aeneid VII. 188, VIII. 285. Ovid, Fasti III. 259-392; Livy I. 20, 4, 1. 27, 7; Varro, De Lingua Latina VI. 14; joannes Lydus, De Mensibus IV. 49.
56 The Golden Bough, Vol. II. pp. 157-182.
57 Festus: Salias Virgines (Mueller, P. 329).
58 H. J. Rose, Primitive Culture in Italy, p. 96.
59 Servius on Vergil's Aeneid VIII. 110.

CHAPTER VI FOOTNOTES

1 See W. Warde Fowler, The Religioms Experience of the Roman People, pp. 185-187.
2 See F. B. Jevons, The Idea of God, p. 115ff.
3 Fasti VI. 155-162.
4 Apuleius, Apologia XLVII.
5 I. 8, 17-23.
6 Naturalis Historia XVIII. 41-42.
7 Macrobius, Saturnalia I. 12, 31-33; see C. G. Leland, Etruscan Roman Remains, P. 108.
8 Marcellus, De medicina XXXVI.
9 Macrobius, Saturnalia 1. 12, 31-33.
10 Ovid, Fasti IV. 911.
11 Ovid, Fasti V. 681-682.
12 I. 24, 7.
13 Livy I. 32, 10.
14 Livy I. 12, 5.
15 Cato, De Agricultura CLX.
16 I. 2. 41-62.
17 I. 20, 4.
18 Ovid, Fasti 111. 323-325.
19 See Pease's note on Cicero, De Divinatione I. 57, 129.
20 See Lucan, Bellum Civile VI. 685-686.
21 Cicero, De Divinatione I. 57, 129.
22 Epistulae I. 16. 57-62.
23 II. 1. 84.
24 X, 289-292.
25 II. 6.
26 Epistulae Morales X. 5.
27 Plutarch, Nyma X.
28 Fasti III. 323-325.
29 Fasti I. 631-632.
30 I. 2. 54.
31 Ovid, Fasti IV. 777-778.
32 The Religious Experience of the Roman People, p. 187.
33 Carmen Saeculare 13-16.
34 Sermones II. 6. 20-23.
35 XI. 2.
36 Saturnalia III. 9, 10.
37 On Vergil's Aeneid II. 351.
38 Cato, De Agricultura, CXXXIX.
39 See Cato. De Agricultura CXXXIX.
40 VI. 390-392.
41 On Vergil's Aeneid IV. 493.
42 XXVIII. 14-15.
43 Aeneid II. 535-539.
44 Aeneid VIII. 484.
45 Aeneid IX. 625-629.
46 III. 8, 13-14.
47 II. 22, 2.
48 See VI. 385-388; X. 23-25; X. 289-292.
49 Satyricon LXXXVIII.
50 Persius II. 3. 16.
51 Juvenal X. 243-245.
52 Juvenal IX. 137-140.
53 See, for example, Lucan, Bellum Civile VI. 523-526.

CHAPTER VII FOOTNOTES

1   Chapter 1, pp. 16-24.
2   Edward Clodd, Animism, p. 22.
3   Chapter 1, p. 23.
4   Genesis XXVIII. 11-18.
5   Joshua XXIV. 26-27.
6   Pliny, Naturalis Historia II. 149-150.
7   A. B. Cook. Zeus, Vol. I. p. 520.
8   Lactantius, Divinae Institutiones I. 20.
9   Pliny, Naturalis Historia 11. 115.
10 Livy XXIX. 10 and 14.
11 See H. W. Howes. in Folk Lore XXXVIII (1927), p. 358.
12 Naturalis Historia XXVIII. 33.
13 See Chapter IV, pp. 133-135.
14 See review of J. P. Mills. The Ao Nagas, in Folk Lore XXXVIII (1927). P. 94.
15 Livy I. 10; Dionysius of Halicarnassus II. 34.
16 Festus: Lapidem silicem (Mueller, p. 115).
17 Livy I. 24. 4-9.
18 Servius on Vergil's Aeneid XII. 206.
19 Siculus Flaccus in Gromatici Veteres I. 141; the complete Latin text is to be found in Frazer, The Fasti of Ovid, Vol. II, p. 483, note 1. See also Dionysius of Halicarnassus, Antiquitates Romanae II. 74; Augustine, De Civitate Dei IV. 23; Fowler, The Roman Fertivals, pp. 324-327.
20 See F. B. Jevons, The Idea of God in Early Religions, p. 21.
21 For the Festival of Terminus see Ovid, Fasti II. 639-684; Horace, Epodi II. 59-60; Dionysius of Halicarnassus, Antiquitates Romanae II. 74; Festus: Terminus (Mueller, p. 368).
22 Plutarch, Quaestiones Romanae XV, Numa XVI. 1.
23 Aeneid VII. 172.
24 Livy IX. 36.
25 Livy I. 31. 3.
26 Vergil, Georgica I, 476-477; see also Pliny, Naturalis Historia XVII. 243.
27 Ovid, Fasti III. 295-296.
28 Naturalis Hisioria XII. 3.
29 I. 1. 11-12.
30 Fronto, Ad Verum Imperatorem II. 6 (Naber, p. 133).
31 De Agricultura CXXXIX.
32 The Fasti of Ovid, Vol, III. P. 352.
33 Florida I. 1.
34 Chapter III, p. 000.
35 H. Dessau, Inscriptiones Latinae Selectae 5047, 5048.
36 Ovid, Fasti II. 67-68, VI. 105-106; Festus: Furvum (Mueller, P. 93). See Georg Wissowa, Religion und Kultus der Romer, p. 236. The ascription of the Festus reference to Helernus depends upon Merkel's change in the manuscript reading Eterno to Elerno.
37 Suetonius, Augustus XCII. 1.
38 See Frazer. The Fasti of Ovid, Vol. II. p. 402.
39 Suetonius, Galba 1. 1 ; Pliny, Naturalis Historia XV. 137.
40 Suetonius, Vespasian, V. 2.
41 See G. W. Gilmore. Animism, pp. 51-58.
42 J. G. Frazer, The Golden Bough, Vol. XI, pp. 160-164; see also Ernest Crawley, Studies of Savages and Sex, pp. 172-173.
43 Festus: Lucaria (Mueller, p. 119).
44 For the Ficus Ruminalis see Livy I. 4, 5, X. 23, 12; Pliny, Naturalis Historia XV. 77; Varro, Res Rusticae II. 11, 5; Varro, De Lingua Latina V. 54; Servius on Vergil's Aeneid VIII. 90; Festus: Ruminalem (Mueller, p. 270) ; Plutarch, Romulus IV. 1; Augustine, De Civitate Dei VI. 10.
45 See Chapter III. pp. 000-000.
46 Suetonius, Caligula XXXV. 3.
47 Festus: Fagutal (Mueller, p. 87).
48 Livy I. 10; Dionysius of Halicarnassus II. 34; Propertius V (IV). 10.

49   III. 25.

50   See Frazer, The Fasti of Ovid, Vol. II, p. 385; Pliny, Naturalis Historia XVI. 235; Festus: Capillatam (Mueller, p. 57).

51   For lucky and unlucky trees see Macrobius, Saturnalia III. 20, 2; Festus: Felices (Mueller. p. 92).

52   See Servius on Vergil's Bucolica I. 52; Horace, Carmina I. 1, 22.

53   Folk Lore XXXVIII (1927), p. 117.

54   Folk Lore XXXVIII (1927), p. 362.

55   Ovid, Fasti IV. 759-760.

56   Seneca, Epistulae Morales XLI. 3.

57   VI. 47.

58   Tacitus, Annales XIV. 22.

59   III. 13.

60   Varro, De Lingma Latina VI. 22.

61   Fasti III. 300-302.

62   For this spring see: Plutarch, Numa XIII. 2; Ovid, Fasti III. 275-276; Juvenal III. 11-20; Livy 1. 19, 5, 1. 21, 3; Festus: Egeriae nymphae (Mueller, p. 77).

63   Frank Granger, The Worship of the Romans, p. 121.

64   Varro, quoted in Servius on Vergil's Aeneid XII. 139.

65   Claudianus, Carminum Minorum Corpusculum XLIX.

66   See Claudianus, De Sexto Consulatu Honorii Augusti 506-514.

67   Pliny, Epistulae VIII. 8.

68   Claudianus, loc. cit.

69   Pliny, Epistulae VIII. 20.

70   Naturalis Historia XXXI. 6-12.

71   Ovid, Fasti V. 673-682.

72   Servius on Vergil's Aeneid VIII. 33.

73   Festus: Peremne (Mueller, p. 245) ; Petronia (ibid., p. 250) Servius on Vergil's Aeneid IX. 24; Cicero, De Natura Deorum II. 3, 9; De Divinatione II. 36. 77. and Pease's note.

74   Apuleius, Metamorphoses I. 13.

75   R. M. Peterson, The Cults of Campania, p. 42.

76   W. Warde Fowler. The Roman Festivals, p. 214.

77   Ausonius, Opuscula X. 379-380.

78   Cicero, De Natura Deorum III. 52; Servius on Vergil's Aeneid VIII. 330.

79   Ethel M. Steuart, The Annals of Quinims Ennims, frag. 19, p. 6; Servius on Vergil's Aeneid VIII. 72; Livy 11. 10; J. G. Frazer, The Fasti of Ovid, Vol. IV. pp. 170-171.

80   Livy, loc. cit.

81   Sermones II. 3, 288-292.

82   Persius II. 3, 16.

83   Tacitus, Annales I. 79.

84   Lily R. Taylor, The Cults of Ostia, P. 34; Local Cults in Etruria, pp. 101-102.

85   C. I. L. p. 336 (second edition).

86   Von Domaszewski. Neptunus auf lateinischen Inschriften in Abhandlung zur romischen Religion, p. 19.

87   See Kirby Smith's note on Tibullus I. 3, 37-40; Vergil, Bucolica IV. 31-33.

88   Cicero, De Natura Deorum III. 20, 52.

89   H. Dessau, Inscriptiones Latinae Selectae, no. 3; Ovid, Fast; VI. 193.

90   Appian, Bellum Civile V. 11. 98.

91   I. 7,26.

92   Festus: Aqua et igni (Mueller, P. 3).

93   See note on Ovid, Fasti IV. 791, in Frazer, The Fasti of Ovid, Vol. III. p. 371.

94   Ovid, Fasti IV. 725-727, 781-782, 805; Tibullus II. 5, 89-90; Propertius V. 4. 75-78.

95   Fasti IV. 785-786.

96   Frazer, The Fasti of Ovid, Vol. III, P. 343.

97   For this rite see Pliny, Naturalis Historia VII. 19; Servius on Vergil's Aeneid XI. 784-785; Silius Italicus V. 175-181; Strabo V. 2, 9; Dionysius of Halicarnassus, Antiquitates Romanae III. 32. Compare Frazer's note on Ovid, Fasti IV. 553; he maintains that Feronia, not Apollo Soranus, was concerned in the rite.

98   According to Servius on Vergil's Aeneid XI. 785.

99 Plutarch, Quaestiones Romanae I.

100 Tibullus 1. 5, 9-12.

101 Ovid, Fasti IV. 739-740.

102 See Frazer's note on Ovid, Fasti IV. 739.

103 Tibullus 1. 2, 61.

104 Plutarch, Quaestiones Romanae 1;
     Varro, De Lingua Latina V. 61.

105 On Vergil's Aeneid VII. 678.

106 Fasti IV. 788.

107 Servius on Aeneid 1. 730. See W. Warde
     Fowler, The Religious Experience of the
     Roman People, p. 73.

108 Fowler, The Religious Experience of the
     Roman People, pp. 136-137.

109 See Ovid, Fasti III. 141-144; Festus: Ignis
     Vestae (Mueller, p. 106) ; Macrobius,
     Saturnalia I. 12, 6; Servius on Aeneid II.
     296-297; Fowler, The Religious Experi-
     ence of the Roman People, p. 136.

110 See H. J. Rose, Primitive Culture in Italy,
     pp. 43-44.

111 Aeneid V. 662, VII. 77; Ennius. quot-
     ed in Festus (Mueller, P. 153) under
     Metonymia; Tibullus 1. 9, 49-50; Fronto,
     Ad Marcum Caesarem IV. 5, 2 (page 68
     in the edition of S. A. Naber).

112 See Lily Ross Taylor, The Cults of Ostia,
     pp. 14-20.

113 Vitruvius, De Architectura 1. 7. 1.

114 Festus: Piscatorii ludi (Mueller, p. 238).

115 De Lingua Latina VI. 20.

116 III. 5, 8.

117 See Frazer, Myths of the Origin of Fire,
     pp. 106 and 226.

VAMzzz Publishing

Paper books

VAMzzz Publishing is located in the very centre of old Amsterdam, in The Netherlands. Our publishing company creates high quality revised editions of five star occult, witchcraft, Gothic and esoteric classics, mostly written in the Fin de siècle-period and early 20th century.

As a publisher, we deeply respect the writer of any book we choose, so we join our forces (top level graphic design & thirty years of occult studies) to produce enchanting volumes which maximize the reading pleasure and inform, often with extra added information. In contrast to the current trend of digital screen addiction, we think, this variety of literature needs to be presented on paper. *No e-books, but real books!*

Apart from republications of valuable but forgotten books, we are also in the preparation of new publications on topics such as self-healing, magic, new astrology and more.

VAMzzz Publishing
P.O. Box 3340
1001 AC Amsterdam
The Netherlands
contactvamzzz@gmail.com
www.vamzzz.com

Previews of all books including a complete table of contents can be viewed on www.vamzzz.com. More books will be added to the list. *VAMzzz Publishing* strives to publish new volumes every month. Please visit our website regularly for the latest updates.

Recommended

**Etruscan Magic
& Occult Remedies**
Charles Godfrey Leland
628 pages, paperback
ISBN 9789492355003
www.vamzzz.com

Etruscan Magic & Occult Remedies by Charles Godfrey Leland was first published in 1892 as *Etruscan Roman Remains in Popular Tradition*. Part One of the book offers complete and detailed insight in the Etruscan and Roman rooted pantheon of the Tuscan Streghe (witches). Part Two describes many of their spells, incantations, sorcery and several lost divination methods.

Leland found himself at the crossroads of the academic and the romantic and it is precisely this, which makes the reading of his work so enjoyable. His primairy aim was to preserve this ancient traditional knowledge, as he feared, it would soon be wiped out by modernism. Much information in this book, Leland received first hand from the Tuscan witches Maddalena and Marietta. His second work on Stregheria: *Aradia, or the Gospel of the Witches* was published seven years later in 1899. One could state he reached his goal as his books are still of invaluable importance to both the Italian folklore and the modern practitioner of witchcraft. One of Leland's readers was the late Gerald Gardner, which makes one wonder who was the true godfather of modern witchcraft…

Chaldean Magic
It's Origin and Development
by François Lenormant
454 pages, Paperback, ISBN 9789492355027

The essentials of magic in Chaldea are presented inside a context of comparison or contrast to Egyptian, Median, Turanian, Finno-Tartarian and Akkadian magic, mythologies, religion and speech. Interesting is the Chaldean demonology, with its incubus, succubus, vampire, nightmare and many Elemental spirits, most of them coalesced with the primal powers of nature.

Aradia
Gospel of the Witches
by Charles Godfrey Leland
174 pages, Paperback, ISBN 9789492355010

This wonderful book describes the creation according to Italian witch-lore. We also read about the witch-meeting or sabbath (treguenda) and the book contains many original magical recipes, like spells for love and good fortune. Diana is further connected to the Moon and the fairy world.

Unicorn
A mythological investigation
by Robert Brown Jr.
124 pages, Paperback, ISBN 9789492355072

Brown Jr. believes the unicorn to be a lunar symbol, and draws on mythology from a wide range of sources all over the world to build his case. The author discusses the heraldic use of the unicorn, relates the creature to ancient goddesses like Astarte, Hecate en the Gorgon Medusa, and provides the reader with lost esoteric Moon-lore.

Là-Bas
A Journey into the Self
by Joris-Karl Huysmans
378 pages, Paperback, ISBN 9789492355058

The plot of *Là-Bas* concerns the novelist Durtal, who is disgusted by the emptiness and vulgarity of the modern world. He seeks relief by turning to the study of the Middle Ages. Through his contacts in Paris, Durtal discovers that Satanism is not a thing of the past but alive and kicking in turn of the century France. The novel culminates with a description of a black mass.

Devil-worship in France
Or The Question of Lucifer
by Arthur Edward Waite
240 pages, Paperback, ISBN 9789492355065

In *Devil-Worship in France,* Waite attempts to discern what is genuine from what is fake in the evidence of 19th century Satanism. To get the answers he spends a great deal of time investigating the French Masonic echelon, debunking a "conspiracy of falsehood" and determining what should be understood by Satanism and what not. Huysmans' diabolical novel *Là-Bas* (1891) inspired Waite to write this sceptical analysis.

Testament of Solomon
A First Century AD Grimoire
76 pages, Paperback, ISBN 9789492355041

A first century AD grimoire, and therefore the oldest, and least known, of all grimoires (magical instruction books) in the occult tradition. The book describes health inflicting demons of zodiacal decans, summoned by King Solomon, and how he controlled them to use their forces to build his temple and more. Translated by F. C. Conybeare, appeared first in the *Jewish Quarterly Review* of October, 1898.

Amazons - *Two publications in one book -*
I. The Amazons by Guy Cadogan Rothery
II. Religious Cults Associated With the Amazons
   by Florence Mary Bennett
328 pages, Paperback, ISBN 9789492355089

Contents I: The Amazons of Antiquity – Amazons
in Far Asia – Modern Amazons of the Caucasus –
Amazons of Europe – Amazons of Africa – Amazons of
America – The Amazon Stones.
Contents II: The Amazons in Greek legend – The Great
Mother – Ephesian Artemis – Artemis Astrateia and
Apollo Amazonius – Ares.

Ophiolatreia
Rites and Mysteries of Serpent Worship
Author: Hargrave Jennings
186 pages, Paperback, ISBN 9789492355126

An account of the rites and mysteries connected with
the origin, rise and development of serpent worship in
various parts of the world, enriched with interesting
traditions, and a full description of the celebrated
serpent mounds & temples, the whole forming an
exposition of one of the phases of phallic, or sex
worship.

Voodoos and Obeahs
Phases of West India Witchcraft
by Joseph J. Williams
374 pages, Paperback, ISBN 9789492355119

This work goes into great depth concerning the New
World-African connection and is highly recommended if
you want a deep understanding of the dramatic historical
background of Haitian and Jamaican magic and witchcraft,
and the profound influence of imperialism, slavery and
racism on its development. Williams includes numerous
quotations from rare documents and books on the topic.

Fairy Mythology *(Volume 1)*
Romance and Superstition of Various Countries 1
by Thomas Keightley
404 pages, Paperback, ISBN 9789492355096

Fairy Mythology *(Volume 2)*
Romance and Superstition of Various Countries 2
by Thomas Keightley
404 pages, Paperback, ISBN 9789492355102

The term Fairy covers all kinds of nature spirits, not just the tiny sugar sweet creatures hovering around flowers. A unique and impressive book on this subject, published in a revised 2 volume-edition. No wiccan or pagan can afford to leave these books unopened. About Elves, Dwarfs, Kobolds, Trolls, Changelings, Meremaids, Nisses, Fairies, Brownies, Puck and other Elemental spirits all over the world.

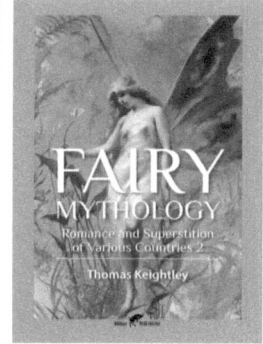

www.ingramcontent.com/pod-product-compliance
Lightning Source LLC
Chambersburg PA
CBHW020243130626
46549CB00005B/2030